War!

War!

The Memoir of a Spanish Soldier Wounded in the Philippines

Ricardo Burguete

Edited and translated by D. J. Walker

Foreword by R. Geoffrey Jensen

HAMILTON BOOKS
Lanham • Boulder • New York • London

Published by Hamilton Books
Hamilton Books is an imprint of The Rowman & Littlefield Publishing Group, Inc.
4501 Forbes Boulevard, Suite 200, Lanham, Maryland 20706
www.rowman.com

6 Tinworth Street, London SE11 5AL, United Kingdom

Copyright © 2020 by The Rowman & Littlefield Publishing Group, Inc.

All rights reserved. No part of this book may be reproduced in any form or by any electronic or mechanical means, including information storage and retrieval systems, without written permission from the publisher, except by a reviewer who may quote passages in a review.

British Library Cataloguing in Publication Information Available

Library of Congress Cataloging-in-Publication Data

ISBN 9780761871392 (pbk.)
ISBN 9780761871408 (electronic)

To their Royal Highnesses

The Most Serene Princes of Spain
Don Alfonso and Don Luis
of Orleans and Borbón

Contents

List of Illustrations	ix
Foreword *R. Geoffrey Jensen*	xi
Acknowledgments	xv
Introduction *D. J. Walker*	1
Chapter 1	15
Chapter 2	19
Chapter 3	25
Chapter 4	31
Chapter 5	37
Chapter 6	41
Chapter 7	49
Chapter 8	53
Chapter 9	57
Chapter 10	61
Chapter 11	65
Chapter 12	69
Chapter 13	73

Chapter 14	75
Chapter 15	77
Chapter 16	81
Chapter 17	87
Chapter 18	91
Chapter 19	97
Chapter 20	101
Chapter 21	109
Chapter 22	115
Chapter 23	117
Chapter 24	121
Chapter 25	123
Chapter 26	127
Chapter 27	133
Chapter 28	139
Chapter 29	141
Chapter 30	145
Bibliography	149
Index	151
About the Editor	153

Illustrations

Figure 1   "Lantana," A small cannon used by Filipino forces against the Spaniards.   136

Figure 2   Chinese transport worker.   136

Figure 3   Map of Cavite Province.   136

Figure 4   General Lachambre and his General Staff.   137

Figure 5   "Victory at Imus."   137

Foreword

One of modern Spain's most fascinating and enigmatic military figures, Ricardo Burguete, was a Spanish war hero who garnered political, professional, and even some literary fame over the course of his long career. He was especially active as a writer during the decade and a half after returning from the Philippines, where his experiences provided him with ample material for this important book. A public figure who gained the attention of such intellectual luminaries as José Ortega y Gasset and Miguel Unamuno, his later writings would cover topics ranging from infantry tactics to Nietzschean philosophy to medieval Spanish religious history. In the process, he disseminated within the Spanish officer corps some of the anti-liberal ideas that eventually found their way into the far right-wing ideology of the dictatorship of Francisco Franco, even though he himself ended up on the other side of the political spectrum. The ideas of anarchism, proto-fascist modernism, socialism, and other widely varied movements influenced him at different points in his life, even as he consistently embraced Spanish patriotic and military values.

He entered the world of the Spanish military as a fourteen-year-old cadet, and shortly after completing his academy studies he fought in Morocco, where he received a prestigious award for combat valor. He was then sent to join the fight against the *independistas* in Cuba, where he—unlike his brother—survived the fighting and disease that took so many Spanish lives. As he writes, not long thereafter he boarded a ship for the Philippines to take up arms once again. Advancing rapidly up the ranks, he would serve as High Commissioner for Africa during a key period in the Spanish-Moroccan War. Later he took command of the Spanish Civil Guard, a militarized police force that was one of the country's most powerful institutions. He culminated his career at the head of the military high court whose actions helped set the stage for the fall of dictator Miguel Primo de Rivera and the subsequent proclamation of Spain's first democracy, the Second Republic. After the republic's founding he loudly proclaimed his intention to join the Spanish Socialist Workers' Party, even though he had once directed harsh military repression against striking workers. In 1936, he strongly condemned the military coup attempt that sparked the Spanish Civil War. In short, neither his political nor his philosophical views fit neatly into one category—a characteristic he shared with others from the European intellectual vanguard but far fewer career military men.

This book, expertly translated into English by D. J. Walker, recounts his journey to the Pacific during the late nineteenth-century Spanish war against Philippine separatists, the political situation he encountered on the islands, the experience of battle, and his near-fatal wounding and painful recovery. He also expresses his ideas on Spain and its future, war, religion, and patriotism, sometimes through the voices of friends and acquaintances who appear in the narrative. As Walker notes in her introduction to this edition of his work, the recurrent themes of the Spanish flag and the cross figure prominently in this book, and the concept of sacrifice brings the two together.

Burguete's vision of Spanish national identity, symbolized by the flag, and his exaltation of sacrifice in battle would continue to surface in his writings for years to come, even as he departed somewhat from his more traditionalist military colleagues when writing about the Church. The flag as a symbol of the *patria* was hardly unique to Spain, but in the world of the Spanish army it was an especially prominent motif. Hence the manual on "military morals" assigned to generations of Spanish infantry cadets included a long passage on the importance of explaining the full meaning of the national flag to conscripts, and the Spanish Foreign Legion would call its battalions, to which the legionnaires professed great loyalty, "flags" (*banderas*). The title of future dictator Francisco Franco's account of his time in the Legion, *Diario de una bandera*, is also telling. As Walker notes in her introduction, Burguete would add a biological element to his description of the Spanish flag, depicting it as a living organism. The biological, often Darwinist, language anticipated some of his later writing. It also highlights how much he had in common with Ramiro de Maeztu and other writers associated with the so-called Generation of '98, whose obsession with national regeneration featured prominently in turn-of-the-century Spanish political and literary circles.

Burguete's views on sacrifice—for military, national, and religious ends—also overlapped with some of Maeztu's writing, although the religious allusions in his writings would become less frequent with time. He came to share with Maeztu a strong interest in the Japanese warrior codes of Bushido, of which self-sacrifice was a valued component. Like Maeztu, Burguete perceived the lessons of the Russo-Japanese War (1904–1905) to be of vital importance for Spain, linking the apparent willingness of patriotic Japanese soldiers to sacrifice their lives in blind frontal attacks against Russian defenders to the regeneration of Japan and its revived status as a formidable military power. Although Burguete was hardly the only soldier to praise death in battle as the ultimate sacrifice for the fatherland, he did so in particularly forceful terms. His descriptions of soldiers proclaiming their love of Spain as they fought and died at the hands of Philippine rebels anticipated the exaltation of patriotic death in battle that became a fundamental tenet of the Spanish Foreign Legion, whose official worldview eventually found a place in the ideology of Franco-ism. Tellingly, the founder and first commander of the Legion, José Millán-Astray, also embraced Bushido, most likely as a result of Burguete's writings on the subject. Burguete described his own combat wound in the Philippines, the pain it caused him, and his subsequent convalescence in a hospital filled with suffering and death in similarly transcendental terms, embracing the trope of "glorious," sacrificial death in battle that the Legion—and later the Franco regime—would associate with patriotism and embrace even more forcefully. The influence of Thomas Carlyle's writings on Norse mythology and "great men" in history also left its mark on Maeztu and on Burguete's account on the Philippines, and it appeared in the Spanish officer's other writings as well—especially his anonymously-written book *Así hablaba Zorrapastro*, which was paradoxically both a satire of Nietzsche's book *Thus Spoke Zarathustra* and an ode to the famous German philosopher.

Burguete's account of the Philippine war thus provides us not only with an engaging account of the conflict from a Spanish perspective, but it also reveals the early intellectual development of a noteworthy figure in modern Spanish history. It betrays its author's background as a largely self-taught thinker and aspiring writer, and it is not difficult to discern from the pages of this book that his formative educational experiences took place in the world of the Spanish army. But as the account of a young officer whose biggest exploits were yet to come, it offers a valuable look at the Philippine Revolution and a crucial chapter in Spanish colonial, military, and cultural history.

R. Geoffrey Jensen
Holder of the John Biggs '30
Cincinnati Chair in Military History
Virginia Military Institute

Acknowledgments

Since I first met Dennis O'Leary in the early 1990s at the Philippine Mission to the United Nations, he has generously provided me with books and articles connected to my research projects. He has also sent me newspaper clippings and his own informal reviews of contemporary books so that I could keep abreast of developments in the Philippines. His encouragement has meant a great deal to me. I am also deeply grateful to Fred Balinong S.J., whose friendship has been invaluable during the last thirty years. Father Freddie has always enthusiastically endorsed my projects related to the Philippines. Even more, he has read and commented on my work as well. I owe both men a huge debt of gratitude.

For several years I have relied heavily on Sylvia A. Macey whose advice and help in the preparation of my manuscripts has been indispensable. I am also indebted to Asma Bouhrass who has resolved difficult questions—such as copyright issues—for me from her service for researchers outside Spain.

Introduction

In the late summer of 1896 twenty-four-year old Ricardo Burguete embarked on a Spanish steamer, the "Alfonso XIII," headed for the Philippines where he was to join the effort to crush the revolution launched by the Grito de Balintawak on August 24, 1896.[1] Ten years earlier, at the age of fourteen, Burguete had enrolled in the Academia General Militar. In 1893, he participated in the Melilla campaign in North Africa. Shortly afterward, he was awarded the Cruz Laureada de San Fernando for bravery in combat in Cuba in 1895–1896 and was duly promoted to captain. Following his stint in the Philippines, Burguete returned to Spain in the spring of 1897 to recuperate from serious wounds suffered in battle. He was awarded the Cross of Maria Cristina and promoted to major.[2]

Most of Burguete's adolescence and adult life was spent in the military. His immersion in the military culture of the 1890s and early 1900s was complemented by wide reading and a desire to make a name for himself as a writer. In the memoir he completed in 1900 and published in 1902 describing his tour of duty in the Philippines, Burguete revealed a literary sensibility rooted in a vivid sensory account of his surroundings along with a notable directness in his descriptions of combat and physical suffering.[3] From his standpoint as a military man and as an intellectual engaged in the issues of his time he commented on a variety of topics in his memoir: the sites he viewed en route, most under British rule; the ethnic and racial groups he observed; Manila and its environs; military engagements he participated in against the insurrectionists; conditions in the hospital where he was treated for the wound he suffered; the Jesuit Fathers with whom he lodged when he left the hospital; the indigenous inhabitants of the islands, the causes of the insurrection; and lastly, the measures Spain should take to remedy the effects of the 1898 Disaster.

Throughout his memoir Burguete focused on the significance and power of two symbols: the Spanish flag and the Christian cross: The flag was, "the greatest symbol there is after the sacrosanct symbol of the cross" (chap. 27). Burguete believed that these two symbols, rightly acknowledged and interpreted by Spaniards, would lead to a sense of the nation and its goals that would overcome the pervasive dismay—especially among intellectuals—that followed the events of 1898.

During his journey and stay in the Philippines Burguete observed the Spanish flags he saw in different circumstances, carefully commenting on the significance of their appearance. Sometimes they flew gallantly on deck as the "Alfonso XIII" ploughed the seas en route to the Archipelago. The sight of the victorious flag flying above the estate house in Imus in 1897 excited the patriotic fervor of the Jesuit friars and military men who witnessed it at Burguete's side. In the company of the friars, Burguete was reminded of the sacrifice of Catholic missionaries, friars, and soldiers who "succumbed amidst rivers of blood to raise the flag on the towers of conquered towns and villages" (chap. 26). These sacrifices merited constant commemoration, he wrote. On other occasions, Burguete observed flags raised on Spanish vessels that fell to the deck for various reasons and lay fluttering, he wrote, like wounded birds. Instances of this distressing phenomenon should serve to remind Spaniards, demoralized by their country's increasing irrelevance in the face of international competition for markets, that success in that competition and victory over colonial rebellions must be pursued even more steadfastly. Regarding the pitiable sight of the flags resembling wounded birds, his fellow soldier, Josep Conangla, took Burguete's anthropomorphizing bent further. He conceived of the flag as an organic entity that bled when the fortunes of Spain were at a low point. In his poem "The Red Mass," Conangla wrote that "from atop a fort, I spied/the red and yellow flag of Spain / whose folds appeared to melt / drop by drop, with blood!" In battle and when he thought about casualties in battle, Burguete likened the color red in the flag to blood but he did not imagine a bleeding flag as Conangla so memorably did in his poem, first published in 1904.[4]

The flag was one of the two essential elements in Burguete's brand of patriotism. The other was the cross. In the last chapter of his memoir, Burguete described a kind of altar or shrine he built for the benefit of his sons that displayed a bit of a Spanish flag and a cross. He hoped to inculcate a reverence for both symbols through a visual, material representation which he obliged his sons to contemplate every day. The link between the two symbols was the concept of sacrifice. Sacrifice for the benefit of the Father or Motherland in warfare and sacrifice understood to elevate an individual's moral and spiritual standing by emulating Christ's sacrifice on the cross.

Burguete's feelings and thoughts about the significance of the Spanish flag and the cross were undoubtedly closely held convictions before he sailed to the Philippines. Everything he encountered on the way and during his stay there contributed to and deepened his concept of the nationalism he hoped to bolster through the power of these two symbols to stir the emotions.

THE JOURNEY TO THE PHILIPPINES THROUGH THE SUEZ CANAL

As Burguete passed by or briefly visited islands or outposts along the route, he commented on many aspects of what he saw, but most significant was his appreciation of the fact that these sites were colonial possessions belonging for the most part to the British. "Between 1880 and 1913, colonized territory more than doubled, from 25 to 53 million square kilometres; as a result, an additional 200 million people came under imperial rule."[5] Nations who could do so were holding onto or acquiring possessions while Spain was in the painful process of losing hers. In Singapore, Burguete wrote that "The commerce of all the strong nations of Europe had many representatives in that vast commercial port. For several hours we took our place among multiple flags from the strong and entrepreneurial countries." Then as the "Alfonso XIII" sailed away, "Above the innumerable masts visible in the port, many flags of all the nations of Europe were floating in the wind. Our flag was unfurled in the stern, and, in its solitary humility, abandoned for the moment by the breeze, it wasn't long before it collapsed. As it folded, it fell onto the deck and there it pulsated like the fluttering wings of a dying bird" (chap. 5). Burguete explicitly connected this sight to the bloodletting Spain was undergoing in Cuba and the fresh wound currently inflicted on it in the Philippines.

Burguete always remarked on the tidiness and cultivated beauty of the English parts of the cities he visited en route to the Philippines. In contrast, he described the filth and lack of sanitation of the places and neighborhoods inhabited by natives or other foreign, non-white residents. Port Said offered the voyagers the first sight of workers—Ethiopians, Berbers, and Egyptians—downloading coal:

> The ferocious visages of that invasion of creatures in tatters were greasy with sweat. Their natural blackness or the dark streaks rolling down their faces caused by sweat and coal dust made the whiteness of their teeth stand out. Their teeth were on constant display because of the tireless mobility of their faces and tongues. With every utterance they spat out a stream of syllables and sounds, which threatened to soil everything—not only with the trace of spit they left in their wake, but also with the stench of their breath that was so dense and strong

it didn't take long to condense, converting their exhalations into grime and grease. (chap. 2)

From the workers on the docks in Port Said, to Aden, to men and women who labored in Colombo in former Ceylon, to beggars everywhere, to Singapore, and finally, to the inhabitants of Manila, Burguete represented dark-skinned natives as different in kind from Europeans. He likened the darkest-skinned individuals to monkeys and chimpanzees. The Chinese were always yellow; in Singapore they were "loathsome, yellow Chinese" (chap. 5). Burguete noted the custom of chewing betel nut enjoyed by the Chinese. When he observed lounging Chinese on the streets of Manila chewing betel nut, he wrote that it "made their faces resemble clowns, or it gave them a look of cannibalistic ferocity" (chap. 6). In Manila, he claimed that it was difficult to distinguish between the faces of male and female *indios* [generally used to refer to indigenous inhabitants of the islands] or they looked alike; identical editions of the same original pair.

Burguete conveyed the strangeness of the inhabitants of the places he visited, never attempting to conceal his distaste for them. His alignment with commonly held views at the time obviated any need to plainly state that the obvious differences in the color, physiognomy and customs of native populations compared to Europeans constituted sufficient justification for their submission to colonial masters.[6] He was somewhat more nuanced in his evaluation of the natives he encountered in Ceylon who came from Indian stock. He mused about how extensive India's dominion might have been had it been able to conquer the plagues and famines it experienced periodically. He did not admire Buddhism (or presumably, Hinduism, which he did not comment on), but he appeared willing to concede the relative value of its traditions, written records, and culture, as he noted in a rather cursory fashion after his visit to a Buddhist Temple in Singapore.

Burguete did not limit himself to personal observations of the people and places he visited. On board the "Alfonso XIII" he read Thomas Babington Macaulay's long essay on Lord Clive, who in Macaulay's view founded British power in India.[7] Burguete strongly approved of Macaulay's depiction of Lord Clive's aggressive nature and his actions in support of Britain's commercial interests in India. Another writer who spoke to Burguete's interest in the keys to successful empire-building was Thomas Carlyle.[8] In his reflections on heroes and heroism, Carlyle extolled valor, seen in earlier times as the essential trait enabling manly action in the world. It was also an indispensable trait in a world of aspiring conquerors. The Norse men Carlyle singled out for their fierce valor were thus an important model for conduct in battle, but they also reminded Burguete of Spain's conquistadores whom he sometimes characterized as intrepid adventurers only secondarily motivated by lust for power and material gain.

At times, Burguete downplayed the stirring adventures of the conquistadores to express regret at the long history of Spanish conquest that did not lead to sustainable enrichment for Spain or for the people it conquered. Depending on the context, whether stressing the beneficial aspects of colonialism or the failure to achieve them, Burguete selectively attributed valor and commercial acumen—or lack of it—to Spanish explorers and the modern Spanish colonial masters of the East and West Indies. Burguete assumed that the British in India and elsewhere invested successfully in the development of the countries they ruled and profited greatly from that investment in the home country. The bestowing of economic gain for all concerned, masters and the indigenous populations they governed, was an important claim to sweeten the imperialistic drive at the heart of contemporary nationalism.[9] Burguete made it clear that in his view colonizers and colonized in the places he visited were in conformity with the rational, natural mandate governing the exercise of power. In short, he thought that Spain did not exploit its colonies nearly as advantageously as Britain did. His opinions as to why this was so did not change appreciably during his stay in the Philippines.

BURGUETE'S ARRIVAL IN MANILA

On his arrival in Manila, Burguete took full advantage of the opportunity to explore the city either alone or guided by a friend. He praised the amenities of his hotel in the Tondo neighborhood, the Bridge of Spain, Intramuros, designed by Miguel López de Legazpi in 1571 with its shady, tree-lined streets, convents, and Cathedral. Outside Intramuros, he admired the chalets of affluent owners, located along the banks of the picturesque Pasig River crisscrossed by many different kinds of vessels. He also praised the tall, grand buildings located on the Escolta where European commerce was conducted. An excursion to the malecon took him through neighborhoods whose attractive houses were shaded by exotic plants. The evening promenade as he reached the malecon was made more enjoyable by the sight of young ladies taking the air in slow-moving coaches. There were refreshments and music on offer. Then, and in the drive to La Luneta, the atmosphere of the entire outing, despite the dust kicked up by the horse-drawn coaches, was suffused with the scent of sweet-smelling plants and refreshed by light breezes.

The Chinese quarter, which he visited alone, presented a sharp contrast to the European or Europeanized parts of the city and its immediate environs. Yellow, sickly looking Chinese slumped indolently at the front doors of their hovels or shops smoking opium and chewing betel nuts. He noted that the shops owned by the Chinese were full of customers. As was the case in the other "native" quarters in cities he visited en route to the Philippines, he registered their presence and in some instances remarked on their work as longshoremen or in the tourist trade—they sold "trinkets" in their shops—without further discussion of their place or impact on the economic life of the cities they inhabited. Burguete did not linger long in this part of the city that reeked of acrid, spicy odors. The only other references he made to the Chinese in his memoir from that point on pertained to their employment by the Spaniards as porters of military supplies, including foodstuffs.

MILITARY ENGAGEMENTS WITH THE ENEMY

In chapter 11, Burguete explained that he did not keep a complete diary of operations for the three months spent around the town of Dinalupijan. "Therefore," he wrote, "I can only give you colorful impressions, faded inevitably by the undertow of time." However, with this exception, in chapters 8–18 he described preparations for fighting and actual combat, noting in great detail the challenges presented by the terrain, the heat, and the sun. He described the effort required in marching through the soft, uneven soil of fields whose crops had recently been harvested, through mountainous territory, and jungles. The oppressive heat and the blinding sun tried the men's endurance. They were also constantly worried about the crowds of indigenous men and women they encountered in villages on their marches who might turn against them at any time. This concern applied as well to the indigenous soldiers fighting alongside them. Burguete further emphasized the fatigue his men experienced in pursuing an elusive guerilla-trained enemy that disappeared into the countryside to avoid engagement, as had happened in Cuba.

Four of the chapters dedicated to military action (11, 12, 16, and 17), convey the "colorful impressions" Burguete referred to as he began this section of the memoir. Chapter 12 details a very difficult landing on a beach near Morón, an important site of resistance. A battle ensued that left some troops wounded and one Spaniard dead. Burguete supervised the burial of the soldier on the beach not far from the town. "Dripping blood and mud, the broken body rested at the bottom of the grave. Before throwing sand over it, I ordered the company to pray over the body of the comrade who was going to be left behind forever." The soldier's sacrifice was treated with appropriate religious solemnity and was recalled more than once in the course of Burguete's memoir.

Chapter 16 offers vivid impressions of a scene depicting preparations for combat as well as an extensive description of the narrator's state of mind when he was on the brink of combat. Burguete described the Spanish and indigenous troops camped along the Pasig River a few miles from Manila. He enlisted all his senses to portray the heat, the dust and smoke, the sounds, the smells, and the febrile atmosphere enveloping the men and animals gathered there. The following two paragraphs describe the catalysts that transformed the narrator into a Norse man lusting to kill:

> In the evening as the waters of the Pasig River reflected fiery-red clouds, the auxiliary Chinese brigade[10] passed in front of my lodgings carrying on their shoulders pieces of quartered cattle gushing blood. The brigade distributed the meat to the soldiers, and for a long time there hung in the air of the reddish twilight a nauseating odor of skinned flesh and slaughter. In a corral that spread out before me, the cattle belonging to the infantry rubbed against each other and pawed the ground impatiently, and farther off four shining bronze cannons with threatening pendants, were lined up correctly, watched over by two sentinels.
>
> Within sight of the ground stained with blood that was beginning to disappear under the foot traffic, in the midst of the burning heat filled with cries, sharp notes of cornets and out of tune bugles, breathing the dusty air impregnated with the stench of slaughter, I felt the heat of an ardor identical to that of the groups of soldiers rise up from the depths of my being, and the residue of the primitive beast, the ebullience of the *norso* [Norse man] caught fire in my blood and coursed through my arteries, urging me to destroy, to shout, to commit acts of savagery.

The scene before him and his surrender to the reverie it inspired led Burguete to allow that the bellicosity of the Norse men lives on in all of us. But Burguete further reflected that the Norse men had a religion that exalted valor in war for its own sake, complete with Valkyries who carried off to a better place valiant men who had sacrificed themselves heroically. His somber conclusion: "I returned to reality, forgetting the legend of the Valkyries. Humanitarian, pious civilization discarded the pagan fantasy, but it could not discard war. It taught that it was fitting only for vultures and crows—which were at the time puffing up their feathers on the roof of my lodging—to visit men killed in combat, to approach the heaps of the dead and peck indiscriminately at the glassy eyes of their purplish, bloodied corpses."

This was an inadmissible outcome. How to avoid such desecration and honor the sacrifice of the dead was essential to the vision of nationalism that Burguete ultimately offered his readers.

Chapter 17 presents a prolonged account of the terrible thirst Burguete and his men suffered on a long march through the desert in pursuit of the enemy and always in view of the Laguna de Bay. Burguete's parched throat tormented him to the point that he stopped registering his surroundings and gave free rein to his imagination: "with the kind of fictions dreamed up by a somnambulist, I walked on for a distance. My imagination drank in the lake; first I wet my lips, then I took small sips and finally, not satisfied with single draughts of sweet, crystalline water, I drank entire waves, and finished by drinking up the source of the water and drinking mud instead. My ears began to buzz and I noticed sharp pains in my tonsils that moved up into my ears."

The last scene of warfare in the memoir marked the end of Burguete's active participation in the effort to quash the Katipunan rebellion.[11] The chaotic scene of combat in chapter 18 opens with the consequences of brush fires lit by the enemy:

> Suffocation on our return cost the lives of more men than those who would have died defending the town. On the Chinese brigade alone, in charge of transport, death feasted greedily.
>
> __Opium! Opium! *Señolía*, and suddenly taking on the yellowish color of amber, they lay down, their bodies rigid on the ground, and we had to put them on the backs of mules to get them away from the fires the enemy had just lit.
>
> A death without glory, without sacrifice, with no other effort expended than that of life escaping abundantly through their pores since it couldn't leave through their suffocated breathing. The Valkyries would certainly not come to take away the most glorious of those prosaic dead men. Not even the vultures or crows that followed us on the march dared to venture into the dense layer of smoke that enveloped us.

When the battle was fully engaged, Burguete conveyed the pandemonium he experienced as the repetition of the cry "Onward!" drove the men forward: "The most high-spirited men were shouting and echoing the command.... Suddenly, at the same time, an unexpected enormous explosion that vomited fire in our direction provoked a storm of steel that ripped open the ground at our feet, Another blast followed . . . and another." The enemy was momentarily repelled, but shortly afterward Burguete was shot in the leg. He tried to continue the march to meet up and seek help from a nearby Spanish column but: "crazed by pain, and debilitated during the march by my loss of blood, I felt my legs give way, and fearful that the bone was completely fractured, I called a halt and grabbed the shoulders of one of the sharpshooters in the very moment when I was overwhelmed by a hum that sounded like blood boiling in my arteries, and drenched by the cold sweat of the anguish that consumed me, I lost consciousness of space and light."

In the passages quoted above, which described the nightmare of combat, Burguete personalized the abstract concept of sacrifice he had referred to up to this point to focus on the pain he himself suffered as he was in danger of sacrificing his life. The intense pain entailed in the sacrifices he and his fellow Spaniards suffered becomes the dominant theme in the following section set in a Manila hospital.

IN A MANILA HOSPITAL

Burguete's treatment in a Manila hospital gave him the opportunity to praise the doctors and nurses who worked there. He described the Sisters of Charity as solicitous but tough-minded when it came to disciplining their patients. The doctors were competent and even compassionate at times. The officers' hall where Burguete was lodged was clean, the food good. Burguete described the instruments, disinfectants, and medications at the disposal of the medical staff. The principal drawback was the swarm of mosquitos that plagued everyone. Later on in his stay when the insurrection was gaining strength, the indigenous employees in the hospital disappeared one day, leaving the medical and nursing staff in confusion and forced to work even harder despite the increasing numbers of wounded soldiers arriving every day. The flight of indigenous employees underscored the perceived deceitfulness of the natives.

The emphasis in the chapters based on Burguete's hospital stay was on pain: his own pain and the pain of other men. Morphine was administered at times on request, but not as often as the men may have wanted. The stark descriptions of unbearable pain expanded Burguete's representation of soldiers fighting for Spain. They were not only men whose courage in battle he exalted: they were vulnerable creatures, martyrs to duty whose suffering Burguete depicted in vivid terms. An officer in an adjoining bed whose knee had been shattered by a bullet cried out as the doctor examined him: "Ay! Doctor. For your mother's sake . . . tomorrow. Let me rest, My God! . . . The group of heads around the bed drew closer . . . we could hear heartbreaking supplications, muffled sobs . . . laments that released the dolorous turmoil of his guts. . . . Ah, no! Not there, not there, my God! . . . let me be for a moment . . . and after a sharp, piercing cry that reverberated in all the corners of the hall, we heard a hoarse, dry rattling in his throat that opened up the circle of nurses and led the doctor to look for a sedative on the table." While Burguete was as realistic in his descriptions of physical pain as any naturalist writer of the period, he also entered a note of psychological realism when he averred twice in this section that observing another man's pain alleviates one's own. Above all, he sought to underscore the suffering that sacrifice to the cause of Spain exacted.

REHABILITATION IN THE COMPANY OF JESUIT FRIARS

Burguete's account of his stay in a Jesuit convent in Manila overflowed with praise for the hospitable treatment he received there. It allowed him to counter the opprobrium heaped on the friars in the Philippines before, during and after his period of service in the Archipelago. He did not note that for some foreign and native witnesses—including José Rizal, whom he never mentioned—the Jesuits were often judged separately, and more favorably, than the friars in general.[12] For the most part, Burguete did not explicitly contest the accusations leveled at the friars—their disregard for the welfare of the indigenous people; their immorality; their greed; their refusal to elevate their parishioners through meaningful education; and so on. He chose instead to emphasize the piety of the Jesuits whom he knew at first hand and their willingness to sacrifice their lives for the cross.

When Burguete described the small room he was given in the convent, he set the tone for his subsequent appreciation of the Fathers:

> The dominant color of the bed I was to sleep in was ermine white. Its extreme narrowness continuously reminded the body and spirit of the idea of chastity and celibacy, making any sinful dreams impossible on a cot that scarcely provided enough room to support oneself on the sides of the bed so as to turn over.

A table with devotional material, straight-backed chairs, a lounging chair on one side, and pictures of miraculous stories from the Bible and devout legends completed the furnishings of the room which, without any luxury whatsoever, breathed blessed quietude, solemn retreat, and mysterious devotion.

Once their piety and their [and his] chastity was established, Burguete described some of the pictures he had referred to on the walls of his room and elsewhere in the convent—pictures that depicted acts of self-sacrifice on the part of Jesuit missionaries from the time of the conquest and later. Their patriotic fervor was underlined as convalescents and friars together watched events unfold near Imus with a telescope brought from the Fathers' laboratory.

Exegesis of the principal theme of Burguete's memoir—the glorification of sacrifice to the fatherland, manifested in devotion to the flag and to the cross— largely omitted any opinions of his own on the controversies swirling around the friars' role in the social and political life of the Archipelago. The principal issue was the conflict between the friars and Freemasonry. Banned by the Spanish government in 1896, Freemasonry was considered the source of the insurrectionist ideology of the Katipunan. An article published in the official organ of the Filipino Masons resident in Spain, *La Solidaridad*, laid out the terms of the dispute from the insurrectionists' point of view: "Masonry will exist as long as there is tyranny, for Masonry is but an organized protest of the oppressed. And tyranny will prevail in the Philippines as long as the government remains in the hands of the friars at the service of their interests. For that reason, tyranny in the Philippines is synonymous with the oligarchy of the friars, and to fight against the tyranny is to fight the friars."[13]

Burguete did consider the role of Masonry in the colony, but not in his own words. He paraphrased the words of his friend Argüelles (perhaps his fictional proxy) in a conversation they had while the narrator was in the hospital. In an overall summary of the failures of Spain's occupation of the colony, Argüelles reviewed the challenge to the religious orders by Freemasonry. In effect, he accused politicians in Spain of misunderstanding the effects of the friars' control over the people, who, in fact, were capable of distinguishing between the true import of Christ's words and actions from the emphasis on discipline and punishment imposed by the Friars.

CAUSES AND REMEDIES FOR SPAIN'S LOSS OF THE COLONIES

Two conversations with men who had long experience in the Philippines set out their views on why Spain had failed to maintain its colony. Argüelles and the landowner who figured in chapters 9 and 14 expressed the disappointment of men who had spent most of their lives in the Archipelago and felt that, in the end, Spain's politicians had betrayed their efforts to contribute to the country while advancing their own interest. The failure of Spain's capitalists to invest in the colony's economy and commerce, cupidity, reliance on the friars to control the people—these were the causes of decline. In addition, when it came time to rely no longer on the friars' control and the military was called on to resolve the problem, the mode of recruitment was counterproductive. Men were recruited who did not know why they were being sent to Cuba or the Philippines. Since that was so, they were not an efficient fighting force: "The colony, removed from capital, from industry, from commerce, serving for a long time as the garbage dump of the dregs of the Peninsula or the means to satisfy political concupiscence fostered by the Motherland, living amidst the opposing sentiments of the sectarians, finally exploded and angrily decided to seek purity" (chap. 21).

Burguete advanced the same reasons for the failures of the Empire in the two Indies in chapter 5 as the "Alfonso "XIII" approached Manila. This appraisal, solidified before he reached the Philippines, suggests that he spent little time investigating or entertaining further explanations during the months he spent in the country. However, en route to his posting described in chapter 7, Burguete did comment on the shacks he passed lining the roadway. He then reflected on the four centuries of "misery and hunger" that the numerous pages of the catechism had failed to ameliorate for the masses who were now joining the Katipunan uprising. This was a rare acknowledgement on his part of the friars' role in keeping the common people in hopeless poverty.

CONSUMMATUM EST

In 1900, Burguete finished the last chapter of his memoir titled "Consummatum est,"[14] presumably not knowing or caring to comment on the fact that Rizal was also said to have evoked the last words of Christ four years earlier, on December 30, 1896, as he stood before the firing squad that executed him for fostering rebellion against Spain. While Rizal's personal striving for the goal of independence was over, Burguete's recognition that the colonies were lost set him on a new path. At the end of his memoir, like some of his contemporaries, he referred hopefully to ideas in circulation concerning regeneration.[15] He did not define what he or his contemporaries meant by regeneration. In general terms, it seemed to signify for most of them a program for Spain's return to prominence in the world through a reassessment of its history and an analysis of the "national character." As part of that effort, Burguete advocated promotion of the sources of genuine nationalism: a deep understanding of sacrifice, embodied in the flag and the cross.

A speech by William II in which the Emperor extolled the dead—both French and German who died in 1870–1871—bolstered Burguete's plan to make commemoration of the dead in battle an essential part of efforts toward regeneration. He copied the speech and his reaction to it before he ended his memoir by describing his own efforts to bring about regeneration or redemption as he envisioned it. The shrine he built in his house with bits of the Spanish flag and the Cross was to be the site for daily remembrance of men who had died for Spain. Observance of this ritual on a personal level for the edification of his sons showed the way, in his view, to repentance and reform on the national level.

NOTES

1. On August 23, 1896, members of the Katipunan in Balintawak rose up in arms against the Spanish government. The government's discovery of the Katipunan's existence determined their decision to launch the insurrection at that time. See also chapter 7, n1.

2. See R. Geoffrey Jensen's *Irrational Triumph: Cultural Despair, Military Nationalism, and the Ideological Origins of Franco's Spain* (Reno: University of

Nevada Press), 31–33, 186–88, and 192n4; for information culled from the Archivo General Militar in Segovia on Burguete's career in the Spanish Army. Ricardo Burguete is one of four officers in the Restoration Army who figure in Jensen's study for their influence on military culture in Spain up to and after the Civil War.

3. As the translator of this memoir, I will only note that like many of his contemporaries in the late nineteenth century, Burguete wrote long sentences that I have had to break down in many passages. His most noteworthy stylistic trait is his use of the pathetic fallacy and of rather startling metaphors. For example, he perceived the knotholes in the window frames of his hospital room as weeping eyes. Or, he wrote that a departing ecclesiastic left on his quarters "a stamp of beatitude and order similar to that of a cell impregnated with monastic purity." Chapter 16 is a good example of his narrative skill at setting a scene and steadily building the action to an emotional climax.

4. The original title of "The Red Mass" in Catalan is "La missa roja." The poem was published in the magazine *Joventut* 5, no. 222 (May 5, 1904): 292.

5. From James Sheehan, "Echoes from the Far Side," review of *The Pursuit of Power: Europe 1815–1914*, by Richard J. Evans, *London Review of Books* 39, no. 20 (October 19, 2017): 21.

6. See D. J. Walker, *The Cuban and Philippine Insurrections on the Spanish Stage, 1887–1898* (Tempe, AZ: Bilingual Press, 2001), 88–107, for a discussion of Spanish racial stereotypes during the period in question.

7. Thomas Babington Macaulay, "Lord Clive," in *Critical and Historical Essays*, Volume 1 (first published 1843; Project Gutenberg 2016) http://www.gutenberg.org/ebooks/2332.

8. Thomas Carlyle, *On Heroes, Hero-Worship, and the Heroic in History: Six Lectures* (London: James Fraser, 1841).

9. It is noteworthy that Burguete did not join some of his contemporaries in claiming that colonization benefitted indigenous people by civilizing them, and, in particular by Christianizing them. Judging by the comments in his memoir, Burguete would have acknowledged as accurate and realistic the first part of the following statement: "As late as 1928, Baldwin's home secretary Sir William Joynson-Hicks, the notorious 'Jix,' said: I know that it is said in missionary meetings that we conquered India to raise the level of the Indians. That is cant. We conquered India as an outlet for the goods of Britain. We conquered India by the sword, and by the sword we shall hold it. "So much for the *mission civilisatrice*" in Ferdinand Mount's review "Umbrageousness," *London Review of Books* 39, no. 17 (September 7, 2017): 7.

10. See chapter 16, n1.

11. See also chapter 7, n1.

12. José Rizal, who studied with the Jesuits for five years at the Ateneo Municipal de Manila, wrote in his diary: "I owe a lot to this religious order: almost everything that I am and have." To a correspondent he wrote: "They taught us what was beautiful and the best" in Raúl J. Bonoan, S.J., *The Rizal-Pastells Correspondence: The Hitherto Unpublished Letters of José Rizal and Portions of Fr. Pablo Pastell's Fourth Letter and Translation of the Correspondence, together with a Historical Background and Theological Critique* (Manila: Ateneo de Manila University Press, 1994), 8.

See also John Foreman, F.R.G.S., "Preface to the Third Edition," in *The Philippine Islands* (1905) 3rd. ed. (London: T. Fisher Unwin, 1906; Project Gutenberg 2007), http://www.gutenberg.org/ebooks/22815: "My criticism of the regular clergy applies only to the four religious confraternities in their lay capacity of government agents in these Islands and not to the Jesuit or Paul, who have justly gained the respect of both Europeans and natives; neither is it intended in any degree as a reflection on the sacred institution of the Church," p.vii. In the chapter "The Religious Orders," Foreman wrote: "The Jesuits, compared with the members of the other Orders are very superior men, and their fraternity includes a few, and almost the only, learned ecclesiastics who came to the Colony. Since their return to the Islands (1859) in the midst of the strife with the Religious Orders, the people recognized the Jesuits as disinterested benefactors of the country" (199–211, at 206).

13. *La Solidaridad*, quoted in section "Lodges Form Regional Grand Council," in "History of Philippine Masonry," *Philippine Center for Masonic Studies*, n.p., http://www.philippinemasonry.org/philippine-masonry-from-barcelona-to-manila-1889-1896.html.

14. Christ's last words as quoted in the Bible, John 19:30, translated as "It is finished" (NIV).

15. In Geoffrey Jensen's "Recepción literaria y cultura bélica: la generación del 98, Ricardo Burguete y el nacionalismo militar en España," *Bulletin of Spanish Studies* 84, no. 7 (2007): 871-88, he established the connections between the so-called Generation of 1898 writers and military men interested in examining the ideas encompassed in the term "regeneration." In Spain, advocates of regeneration began to disseminate their ideas even before the Disaster of 1898. For a discussion and listing of books and articles on this subject that Burguete could have had access to before he completed his memoir, see Sebastian Balfour, *The End of the Spanish Empire, 1898–1923* (Oxford: Clarendon Press, 1997), 64–91.

Chapter One

As I paced the deck that morning, in the distance on the starboard side I saw dark spots on the sea's smooth surface marking the Balearic Islands.

At that moment the "Alfonso XIII" was navigating a sleepy, smooth Mediterranean Sea unruffled by the slightest current of air. The kiss of coastal breezes and the amorous sighs drawn from inlets by the bold and intimate caresses of the waves were prevented from reaching us by our distance from land.

The sun was splendid in a sky of limpid blue. It was mirrored by the wide expanse of the sea which at present quieted the capricious storms and squalls befitting a Levantine Othello with its trio of sultanas: France at the head, Spain and Italy pressed jealously to its sides.

The sea kept a protective watch, gathering together the favored islands of its harem in a tender and affectionate embrace: the Balearic Islands, Corsica, Cerdeña, Sicily, Candía and, at its feet, Cypress off in a corner, sleeping through its oriental somnolence, unaccustomed to the uses and habits of its companions.

Sailing directly toward the Suez Canal, we could barely make out the coasts of Corsica, and nearer to us, Sicily. But decency and modesty threw a veil over the still distant islands, so that we could barely make out the pregnant contours of Sicily's mountains, among whose enormous bellies we spotted the prominent silhouette of Mt. Etna.

Flocks of seagulls greeted us courteously as we approached the coast and, after crossing from one side of the ship to the other with self-interested curiosity, disappeared into the distance with shrill cries and frequent dips into the water. Against the horizon the lateen sails of innumerable fishing boats resembled an orderly file of white birds, grave and immobile at our passing, absorbed with the equally absorbed and contagious serenity of the sea and sky.

We sailed at fourteen miles an hour toward Port Said and the entry to the Canal—the first stage of the sea route to the Philippines.

It was impossible to amuse ourselves with the view of the far-off coast whose enormous distance from us ate up sound, color and form.

The uniform smoothness of the water was broken two or three times with the brownish sails of an occasional large boat fishing a mile or a mile and a half from our position. The presence of such boats attracted many curious passengers and was sufficient to cut off access for a long time to the side of our ship where people gathered.

The boats provided a moment's distraction to ward off the tedium of the peaceful hours of the passage, a tediousness further aggravated by the enormous crowd on the ship.

Although the steamship was one of the largest in the *Transatlantic* fleet,[1] the first and second class cabins were completely filled.

Improvised bunk beds had been arranged in all the cabins in such a way as to take up the space next to the door that allowed entrance into the room. It was necessary to take turns to get down or climb up onto those shelves that passed for beds.

My relations with my bunk were so formalized and my ability to stretch out so compromised by its paltry dimensions that I soon abandoned the discomfort of this arrangement—which, in addition, required a respectful pause beforehand at the entrance to the cabin—and decided to accommodate myself at night on one of the benches on deck. Some of the other travelers imitated my example and very soon our good humor earned us a label that was readily accepted due to the boredom of the journey. Everyone used the word from that time on: we were the *golfos* [vagabonds], on board.

With our blankets slung over one shoulder and a pillow under our arms, our nightly appearance before the groups on deck was always greeted with the same phrase:

"Here come the vagabonds!"

I ended up approving of the name given to our late night Bohemia and, joining those amusing groups of fellows I met on the journey, I wrapped myself in my blankets on a narrow bench that allowed me to stretch out in all sorts of extravagant postures in exchange for putting up with its discomfort.

I spent the first nights of the journey on that improvised bed on deck, at the foot of the wheelhouse, a place accessible only to the generals aboard the expedition.

Those were quiet, melancholy nights in which the body surrenders to the day's laziness and laxness. Daily impressions no longer engage the imagination, while thought reveals memories stored in the dark chamber of forgetfulness.

The large number of passengers, which was composed of various groups, was up between eleven and twelve at night when the most numerous single group appeared, composed of all the women on board. From the outset, because they were relatively few they had felt an instinctive need to band together.

From my observation post as I lay on the bench, I heard the happy laughter of the women and the murmur of whoever was speaking. When the speaker suddenly became quiet, the women broke out in explosions of laughter.

My senses were lulled by memories of the past or attuned only to the propeller's rhythmic throbbing. I opened my eyes and by the light of the few electric bulbs on deck I saw curly-haired female heads shake as the women stifled loud laughter in their handkerchiefs—laughter that died away in lace and batiste cloth with a sound like the soft beating of the waves against the sides of the boat.

Night extended the firmament woven of shadows, and in its depth innumerable stars sparkled, twinkling discreetly and winking knowingly. They were mute witnesses of the loves of that sea which in its somnolent laziness lay embracing its favorite islands, and with insatiable desire kissed the intertwined bodies of its three sultanas: France in the north, Spain and Italy clinging to its sides.

NOTE

1. On the *Transatlantic* fleet: in 1880, Claudio López y Bru (1853–1925), the second Marquis of Comillas, controlled a lucrative shipping business that transported Spanish soldiers to and from Cuba and the Philippines. See Francesc Cabana, *La burguesía catalana: Una aproximación histórica* (Barcelona: Proa, 1996), 65–71. Burguete notes overcrowding on board his outbound ship to the Philippines, but does not refer to conditions on inbound vessels that drew criticism from other sources, including the republican journalist Vicente Blasco Ibáñez who wrote: "Comillas has collected millions of *duros ad majorem Dei gloriam* through his shipping business during this Cuban war, yet the transport of soldiers and sick men on his ships is carried out in the most inhumane manner possible. These voyages would have provided useful lessons to the former slavers of Guinea" (Blasco Ibáñez, *Artículos contra la Guerra en Cuba*, ed. J. L. León Roca [Valencia: León Roca, 1978], 236).

Chapter Two

The principal nemesis of the vagabonds was the early morning swabbing of the deck.

Dawn, resembling a narrow metallic strip, had barely broken in the East when the cleaning crew began to swab down the deck and all its recesses with unlimited fury and ferocious streams of water. Not a single hidden place escaped the meticulous scrutiny of the water or the mop.

We had to wake up in the middle of our sweet dreams and walk to the nearest salon with the uncertain steps of people suddenly roused in the night. There we nodded off in the midst of voices and the infernal sound of mopping. And after a short time—enough for tints of red to appear on the smiling face of dawn—a little bell announcing early Mass abruptly awakened everyone. We gathered up our improvised mats and with eyelids pale and swollen with sleep, we were quickly revived by the fresh odor of wood saturated with humidity and the brisk, acrid morning breezes. We attended a Mass held before the drowsy devotion of the passengers was entirely awakened. For us vagabonds the place and the moment lent a mysterious and virginal freshness to the ceremony. All this was heightened by the splendor of daybreak whose light poured in through the half-open windows, illuminating and fully revealing the dazzling whiteness of the dawn sacrifice of the Mass.

On the fifth day of our journey, Port Said[1] appeared before our eyes against the backdrop of a beautiful sunrise. We were about to enter the head of the Suez Canal, a masterwork inspired by the illustrious conquistador Albuquerque and by Duarte Galván, and fully realized in our time by De Lesseps.[2]

Port Said is located next to ancient Pelusa.[3] It looks vibrant and picturesque to the voyager because it contrasts vividly with the low, sandy lands surrounding the city.

We entered the mouth of the canal and took up our place in the long line of ships lying parallel to the dock.

The task of securing the ship was not yet complete when a huge launch birthed alongside our steamer carrying a loud and heterogeneous, dirty, ragged and multicolored crowd amidst big piles of coal.

With astonishing agility and incredible rapidity an avalanche of Ethiopians, Berbers, and Egyptians shouting as if they were mounting a ferocious attack, invaded the deck, opening the hatches on the sides. They set up the scaffolding and began the process of downloading the coal.

The curious passengers on our steamer formed a group at a respectable distance from the launch. The ferocious visages of that invasion of ragamuffins were greasy with sweat. Their natural blackness or the dark streaks rolling down their faces caused by sweat and coal dust enhanced the whiteness of their teeth. Their teeth were on constant display because of the tireless mobility of their faces and tongues. With every utterance they spat out a stream of syllables and sounds, which threatened to soil everything—not only with the trace of spit they left in their wake, but also with the stench of their breath that was so dense and strong it didn't take long to condense, converting their exhalations into grime and grease.

I cautiously approached the guardrail of the steamer. A big Moor with an apostolic beard and a venerable, patriarchal look about him, was directing the work from the hold of the launch. Whenever a maneuver required the cooperation of a number of workers, he contributed to their efforts with a rhythmic, breathlessly delivered song that ended in a cry meant to boost the common effort. The operation of moving up and down the inclined planks that connected the vessels demanded prodigies of balance and was accomplished speedily.

In the midst of a very fine black dust that was almost dense enough to chew, a swarm of workers were bent over in the bottom of the hold scraping out coal from its corners with shovels. They were clothed in the strangest and most diverse attire: *jaiques*, fezes, turbans, hats, kerchiefs and *zaraguey*.[4] Common to them all were the rags they wore over the rest of their clothing.

The "j" at the end of each syllable in their infernal gibberish made their utterances sound like insults. The gestures of these loquacious speakers lent credibility to that thought of mine; two or three times I expected to see work come to a stop and end in a brutal and bloody battle waged with blows from their shovels.

Among the Berbers, Egyptians and Ethiopians, I saw European faces, faces of our own people, faces I would swear I recognized, and I recalled—as I was deciding whether to go on land—the story of the two travellers from Aragón who witnessed a similar scene:

Chapter Two

"Hey, where do you think that savage over there unloading coal with the kerchief on his head comes from?"

A fellow countryman, from Ricla, at your service—the fellow on the launch standing in a group of Ethiopians responded, smiling politely.

There are three quarters in the cosmopolitan city of Port Said: the European, the Arab and the Jewish. The indigenous population does not live separately but rather mixed amongst the others.

It was necessary to visit them by coach right from the outset because as soon as you disembarked, you faced the natural curiosity of onlookers, and you were further blocked by an excitable swarm of young rascals, speaking an original Volapuk,[5] who offered their services as guides. Second, because the principal avenue of the European quarter, which was converted into an immense bazaar, was impossible to traverse calmly without one or more clerks from each one of the establishments coming out and obliging you to examine their merchandise.

They shouted at you in French, Spanish, Italian, Russian, and Turkish. Ultimately, they howled at you if you didn't willingly consent to look at the excessive number of trinkets, as useless as they were expensive, crammed into the shops, jamming the window displays, and pouring out of the doors. It all ended with your hurting your eyes as you stepped out of the shops; a flood of light and color under the burning midday sun was so intense it inundated the neighboring desert. However unsettled your head was, the intoxication of the fair affected your senses even more. A delirium of a fair, its wares loudly hawked in incomprehensible languages, formless objects on display, all ablaze in overwhelming, bright flames.

Along with other shipmates I took refuge in a flamboyantly advertised café situated on the first floor of a large building.

A female orchestra was playing a cheerful musical andante as we seated ourselves at several tables at the back of the empty, formal salon.

All of Europe was represented on the stage where the women were playing: blondes, women with light brown hair, brunettes. They were tall and short, English women, French, Italian, Spanish, German and Russian. Each one of the different nations lived on in the blue, black and bluish eyes of their representatives. The beloved homeland left behind forever as if by the force of a hurricane-like mundane squall, lived on in their eyes, within the frame of those painted faces, of that dyed hair, those pupils that illuminated the dark circles under their eyes amidst glances of infinite sadness and shining streams of tears.

I drank I don't know what. A lethargic, sickly looking woman, supported on the arm of a skinny adolescent, approached us to gather tips as the orchestra took up a piece that was so sentimental, so infinitely sad that the sobs and pained muttering it expressed were almost enough to make us lay our heads on our arms at our tables and cry.

I fled from the café determined to escape the noise and confusion of the street in the first coach I could find.

I entered the Arab quarter. The ragamuffins at the dock yelled and followed the coaches so closely that it was necessary for two black policemen, whose demeanor was majestic and grave, to strike the ragged following twice.

The Arab quarter like the Jewish quarter exudes misery inside and out. But in the Jewish quarter hygiene required the use of water to conceal the trash momentarily under the mud. As we proceeded, I felt like I was passing through a suburban Madrid neighborhood on a procession day.

As in those Madrid neighborhoods there were taverns everywhere, although the turbans and *jaiques* of the customers seated at grungy tables, engaging in lively conversation, or falling asleep alone in corners as they smoked their hookahs, lent it all a different look.

At the doors of the poor hovels, women of all ages formed animated, idle groups. Their inquisitive eyes were visible and, among the veils that covered their faces, the *anilloso canuto boregheh*[6] mask that completely covers the nose was conspicuous.

Curiosity about us put a stop to their conversations and obliged even the cleanest mothers to suspend the long and bloody task of squashing the lice on the heads of their progeny.

We went down many streets, all alike. At one turn we saw a slender Moorish woman, not lacking elegance and grace, who was lifting her skirts coquettishly, revealing her very attractive legs imprisoned in black stockings, secured at the knees by silky garters and lace, and ending in her feet shod in patent leather shoes.

Cypress, oriental Cypress infected by the coquettish luxe of her companions! When we visited the mosque a long line of the faithful turned toward Mecca, bowing in a variety of postures and genuflections.

We were required to put on enormous esparto slippers to enter the temple. We climbed up the stairs that gave access to the mosque. It was not out of the ordinary. The walls are white and adorned with a fringe of fanciful tiles. An enormous book written in Arabic script, greasy, torn and supported on a lectern contained verses of the Koran, according to the guide, that the faithful customarily read. I thought that was doubtful since the few believers present in the temple at that time were snoring or sleeping off drunkenness rather than reading the big old book. And one of them had just given reliable proof of it, leaving on his *jaique* and on the floor an impression that transcended and was very much at odds in color and in spirit with the scribbled, sage impression of the Mohammedan verses.

We walked down the principal streets. We went out into the poor quarters amid wretched houses painted a red as furious as the redness on the cheeks of its inhabitants—sad Messalinas[7] of hunger and misfortune. We went on to the immense sandy areas on the outskirts where herds of camels were rubbing their humps in the hot sand or going to refresh their mangy and moth-eaten coats in the puddles and springs.

NOTES

1. Port Said was founded by Said, the ruler of Egypt, in 1859. The British entered the city in 1882, beginning an occupation that lasted until the Anglo-Egyptian Treaty of 1936 required the withdrawal of British troops except for a contingent of soldiers that remained to protect the Suez Canal.

2. Afonso de Albuquerque (c. 1453–1515) was instrumental in opening up the Far East to an expanding Portuguese Empire. His European fleet made the first voyage into the Red Sea, which he wished to blockade in an attempt to capture Mecca. His contemporary, Duarte Galvão (1446–1517), also Portuguese, was a writer and chronicler, historian and diplomat who tried unsuccessfully to persuade other courts in Europe to join a crusade. Ferdinand de Lesseps (1805–1894), French administrator and diplomat had the Suez Canal built by the Suez Canal Company. It was inaugurated in 1869.

3. Ancient Pelusium was a port fortress located in the eastern Nile Delta, 30 kilometers from modern Port Said.

4. *Jaique* is a long robe with a hood. With the use of *zaraguey*, Burguete may be referring to *zaragüelles*, the traditional baggy trousers worn by farmers in Murcia and Valencia, from Arabic *saragüells*.

5. In 1880, a German priest, Johann M. Schleyer, constructed the Volapuk language based on English, German, and Latin, meant to serve as an international language.

6. *anilloso canuto* is a boregheh mask. For images of a variety of veils or masks covering the nose, see http://www.alamy.com.stock-photo/boregheh.html.

7. Messalina (c. 17/20–48) was the wife of the Roman Emperor, Claudius. She was said to have conspired against her husband and to have entered into a bigamous marriage for which crime she was executed. Her reputation as a whore derives from the Roman poet Juvenal, who wrote that she worked nights in a brothel.

Chapter Three

The ship went aground twice as it approached the canal waterway. The powerful propeller blades moved us out of the mire after stirring up very fine mud at the bottom that blackened the water.

The canal is 60 meters wide and 8 meters 50 centimeters deep.

The "Alfonso XIII" activated the electric projectors on the prow and in the midst of the serene night the ship glided forward with a gentle, uniform movement along the route marked by the buoys with green and red lanterns.

At lengthy intervals coinciding with the railway stations that lined the canal on our right in the direction of Suez, there were small bays in which, lit by the bright beams of powerful electric spotlights, one could see areas for housing obligatory transit stations that served to regulate the traffic on the canal, accessible to only one vessel at a time.

I had just stretched out on my favorite ledge. The hot *khamsim*[1] rose up from the desert sand; its strong winds agitated the surrounding peace and quiet woven of darkness.

I tried to sleep. The visit to Port Said had the dizzying effect of a kaleidoscope on my senses. I tried in vain to fall asleep; it evaded me nonetheless.

The various groups on deck exchanged impressions about the day we had spent in which the loquacity of the females assembled there stood out.

Half-opening my eyelids, I could see the female passengers' curls and soft features, which had been exposed to the sun and were flushed due to the day's agitation. In the chiaroscuro of the night and semidarkness, their heads formed a happy and lively cluster on which the electric lights shone alternately, highlighting sparks of gold, curls of a brilliant black or bits of velvety, soft skin.

The *khamsin*, blowing across the burning sands, seemed to ignite the tiny embers that sparkled in the firmament.

I let my imagination wander far afield, enjoying its evocation of Biblical passages from my childhood.

Across those same burning sands that extended to the horizon, under the same sky that the winds of the desert seemed to ignite—during nights like these the Israelites, guided by Moses, wandered long days and endless nights in search of the Promised Land.

Infinite providence, in the service of the prophet's magical staff, was able to extinguish hunger and thirst. What Moses could not extinguish was bestial hatred, carnal appetites, and exalted passions that found their prey in the crowded camps on suffocating nights similar to this one when the *khamsin* blew and the starry firmament inhaled the fiery darkness. For that reason he passed down the Decalogue written on the famous tablets. It was a wise law that I tried to recall, fighting against the drowsiness that was overwhelming me.

In the struggle carried on in my mind, fighting against the first stages of sleep, I think that it was the sixth commandment that I babbled between closed lips. Startled, I opened my eyes. In the group closest to me, the owners of curly hair were laughing. I went to sleep lulled by their laughter as well as the other lullaby, separate and inextinguishable, that the waves imitated as they broke against the sides of the vessel.

Much later in the morning, we approached the end of the canal. On both sides the sands extended to the horizon. Wretched camels and their dirty drivers crossed the desert under a fiery sun in search of the distant Arab villages, constructed of tiles and yellow mud, situated in those immense, brownish plains that breathed sterility and death.

At the last transit station a group of young ruffians, who were naked and whose skin was the color of sunburnt mud, followed us along the canal shouting at the top of their voices. They unfolded incredibly thin arms and legs as they ran, leaving an imprint on the ground as faint as if they were spiders.

Suez appeared before our eyes with the freshness of an oasis. A dazzling whiteness spread its way up the flat roofs, the tall minarets, and the towers of the Arab Quarter. This extravagant splash of whitewash contrasted with the agreeable severity of the chalets and European buildings amongst rings of ornamental gardens and bright little plazas of multicolored gardens that supported small stands of acacias and wild figs. Labyrinths of gallant palm trees whose trunks were capriciously intertwined, formed separate clusters of flowers on top that ripened into fruit.

The train to Cairo (*Maweel kahirah*), which was puffing smoke on the vast plain, frightening a loose herd of camels, disappeared in the distance just as we arrived.

Before us lay the barren lower heights of the Arabian cordillera which moistened its arid rock crystal and quartz in the Red Sea.

Chapter Three

The crossing of the sea became increasingly tedious as we sailed on serenely. At first, our curiosity evoked the sacred memories of the Biblical passage: the waters parting to let the children of Israel pass over the dry riverbed. But as the coasts receded from view and in the distance the mountains obscured the evocative silhouette of Mount Sinai, we lost interest in the legend. It once again sank into oblivion and nothing could revive it during those dull days without coasts to look at and distinct stages to measure visually. The sun passed through its stages with the inalterable uniformity of its majestic indifference. It set in Africa amidst clouds of fire to rise again, red and smiling amidst lacy white clouds on Asiatic coasts—the immortal and always filled cradle of the human race.

At the end of the Red Sea the island of Peris[2] partly obstructs the entry into the Gulf of Aden, giving access to it along a narrow canal.

Aden[3] sleeps in the shelter of a rocky cordillera. The British flag flies on a semaphore situated on one of its hills. The town, which arises gradually from the edge of the sea, offers nothing worth noting except for the enormous cisterns that store water for times of drought and the reddish line of barracks situated in the highest part of the city. They are hidden or half protected by fortification works, recognizable by the color of the earth that has been turned over.

Remnants of a shipwreck are visible on the surface of the water in the middle of the rather extensive bay. We anchored close to it and the maneuver had scarcely been completed when a fleet of pirogues surrounded our ship manned by adolescent savages who were half naked, with a variety of facial types.

—Hey! Ahoy! Into the sea! Into the sea!

Some of them climbed aboard bearing tiger skins and a variety of merchandise.

Abyssinians predominated. Most of the men were black, agile and slim, less athletic than men on the western coasts.

Their crisp hair, which was the color of old gold, astonished our passengers. I discovered that they obtained that unusual color by applying a dressing of quick lime to their heads for several days.

The metamorphosis was lasting according to those who were able to recount the process, and the pride that the owners of that reddish tangle of hair, which they thought made them look like English misses (and in our opinion, like monkeys) had no limits. We had them dance and, to the beat of rhythmic clapping, they executed little jumps that ended in pirouettes—no less than what chimpanzees, led through our streets by gypsies, can do.

Beside the ship a ferocious shouting accompanied by a continuous slapping of the water with their oars, called attention to the pirogues.

—Eh! Ahoy! Into the sea! Into the sea!

The diversion was identical to what happens on our coasts. Silver coins were tossed into the sea and the negroes dived in after them.

This distraction attracted the passengers' attention for quite some time. Casting modesty aside, curiosity on the part of the female sex didn't squander the occasion for enjoyment, discreetly ignoring the nakedness of those negroes—some of them quite grown up—who amidst happy laughter that ended in a ferocious gritting of teeth, repeated:

—Eh! Pesetas into the sea! Into the sea!

The swimmers' proposition was interrupted for a moment. A peseta fell into the water and no one ventured to go after it.

The negroes looked fearfully into the water where rough waves were rippling the surface.

We didn't have to wait long for an explanation: an enormous shark showed its back as it surfaced forcefully, and shortly afterwards it overturned one of the canoes.

By way of explanation, they all pointed to a small negro who, sitting immobile in one of the boats, displayed the stump of his leg bitten off not long before in similar circumstances.

There was a lot of confused shouting and a racket made by oars slapping the water before the boys in the pirogues resumed their sport.

When we left Aden to reach the Cape Guardafui,[4] the precipitous, parched coasts of phonolite fell away, lost in the distance. These coasts were made of volcanic rock, formed in the tertiary period, inimical to vegetation, and bathed in their aridity with flaming reflections of a sun that would not be long in setting.

Beneficial rain obstinately refused to fall on those lands and terrible droughts could last there for as long as five years.

I recalled a story that elevated thirst to the height of necessity and French gallantry to the height of resourcefulness.

An English couple lived in Aden during one of the long dry spells. The recently appointed French consul carried with him an invitation from his country to visit the couple. After some ceremonial niceties he was invited to experience an exquisite caravan tea a few nights later.

The English woman could not do without her daily bath and, since water was so scarce, she used her bath water for daily domestic use. On the night when the consul was invited, without notifying the maid in advance and at a moment when water was not available, the maid went to fetch it for the tea from the usual container.

The reader may imagine the English woman's (she was blonde) astonishment when the consul stirring the tea in a very delicate porcelain cup from China, picked out from his spoon a very fine, curly hair the color of old gold . . .

Chapter Three

—What is it? The English woman asked. And as she saw the reflections of that curly hair, a blush rose to her cheeks as swiftly as did the explanation supplied by his good sense.

—It's nothing, señora, the imperturbable diplomat responded. A hair from a camel that brought your caravan tea.

The "Alfonso XIII" entered the Indian Ocean in the late afternoon, sailing toward Colombo.

NOTES

1. *Khamsim* is a dry, hot, sandy wind blowing from the south, in North Africa and the Arabian Peninsula.
2. The island in question is Perim, an English possession when Burguete sailed by it in 1896.
3. Aden was under British administration from 1839–1967 and governed initially as part of British India.
4. Cape Guardafui is a headland in the autonomous Puntland region in Somalia. Italy held sovereignty over the Cape when Burguete described it—one among many possessions governed by European powers which Burguete noted as he made his way to the Philippines.

Chapter Four

The sighting of the Island of Socotora first and then the Maldives[1] momentarily distracted the passengers during the monotonous daily stretches we spent traversing the distance between Aden and Colombo.

Heat and boredom prolonged the evening gatherings on deck, but listlessness and a dearth of conversation replaced the previous animation such that it turned the formerly chatty groups into indolent night birds shifting positions restlessly in their deck chairs.

Day times were not any more amusing. Except for the large, dogged group of gamblers, the other passengers, moving close together, walked impatiently back and forth along the deck, read or slept, or gathered after meals to argue.

Suspicions and antipathies arose that led to hatred. Angry hatred, ferocious, saline hatred with the rare property of evaporating like drops of water when the passengers reached land.

I came upon disputes in corners; hateful glances exchanged in the dining room, in the corridors and even, despite their kindness, in the glances of the weaker sex. At night in the numerous gatherings of passengers, I noted symptoms of the same passion in impertinent laughter, in extreme reserve, and in a mocking tone that underscored the intention of the speakers' words.

The "Alfonso XIII," serene and majestic, cut softly through the water and sent its feathery smoke to the wind, which was forcing the rhythmic song through the tall chimney that the engine intoned in the stern amidst boiling foam.

By the light of a purple and diaphanous dawn we discerned the misty coast of the Punta de Gales. Between ten and eleven in the morning the ship dropped anchor in the port of Colombo.

Colombo is the principal port of the *Singhala* of the Indians, Trapobana of the ancients, and Ceylon of modern peoples.[2]

We were only a sixth of a mile from the wharf and we were permitted to go there after the ritual visit to the Department of Health.

The Malabar[3] oarsmen who took us to the wharf were two stalwart youths with dark, bearded faces whose manly traits contrasted with their hair drawn back in a bun around the head, which was adorned with conch combs. Hair and combs went with the long skirts that covered their legs. But the beards and the manly build of their vigorous bodies were fiercely at odds with their feminine adornments.

After lunch in the restaurant closest to the port, I decided to visit the town with several companions.

Several vehicles appeared to fulfill our wishes. We chose one of them drawn by horses only a bit taller than dogs. We got in after making our way with difficulty through the numerous small coaches with one seat pulled by trotting *indios*. All the different castes of India with their diverse clothing and appearances are represented in that hard, inhuman work: the Vedda, the Sinhalese, the Malay and the *indio*.[4] All of them ordinarily used a cinch with cords to pull the coach.

We traversed the main streets of the European quarter. Along each side of its streets, which are laid out in straight lines, sumptuous buildings and luxurious bazaars stand out, separated by gardens of paradisiacal greenery and beauty.

The outskirts of the town are marvelously, splendidly beautiful. Rows of bananas, coconuts, oranges and guavas were the shortest trees, the median height of that exuberant vegetation in which forests of lovely palm trees, of leafy ebonies, of incorruptible teks [iron tree] milky sandalwood, purple *agaleches*, and gigantic bamboo stand out.[5]

This extraordinary flora surges up in a sea of thick and multicolored foliage. We saw delightful chalets or miserable hovels on either side of the road. The one we were on at the time was very crowded with innumerable small coaches carrying correct Englishmen or irreproachable little Englishwomen who with indifferent glances rode among the lines of *indios* and *indias* with bronzed skin and slender bodies. These people returning from work regularly avoided the coaches by making use of both shoulders of the road. Along a low road that bordered a lake covered with lily pads and lotus flowers beneath a ceiling of branches and interlaced leaves, we came upon the pagoda. It is a vast building rebuilt on ruins. Fragments of gigantic colonnades lie scattered on the ground nearby.

I preferred the beauty on the outside to the contemplation of the jewels and tapestries on the inside.

A porcelain Buddha, swollen and very large, protected in an enormous vitrine, displayed his nude belly with an unusually large navel that our Sinhalese guide pointed out to us with a reverent, religious gesture.

I left the temple within hearing of the guide's tedious explanation. Using words affiliated with all languages, he tried to explain some sentences in an enormous book, scrawled in Pali, titled "Mahawanso,"[6] as I understood it. It is a book that deals with the genealogy of great men, written six centuries before J-C, and replete with epic episodes very similar to those that Homer narrated.

We decided to return without going to the famous cinnamon forest.

The heat was stifling and the rays of the tropical sun in the early afternoon, filtered through the leaves and branches, burned like bands of fire. On our return we noted the multitude of diverse races born in that fertile and bountiful land, all of them displaying the powerful fecundity of continual racial crossing.

Bands of children were hanging on the skirts of clashing colors worn by the *indias* who bared the bronzed skin of their slender legs and arms the color of ivory, encircled with silver bangles and bracelets.

The *indios*, their heads covered with very large, multicolored turbans, moved along at a majestic pace, presenting their bronzed shoulders to the sun, naked from the waist up.

As we approached the town, we contemplated along the way original or undefined types, representative of a variety of races or of puzzling mixtures and origins: the Malabar, the Sinhalese, the Malay, the Hindu—the latter with its multiple varieties, the *bil,* the *gond,* the *kol,* the *koku,* the *puliah,* the *vedda.*[7] These are the various classifications of the great number of human beings that make India the most populated country in the world after China.

Under the hot caress of the early afternoon sun, in the midst of that burning land pregnant with exotic vegetation, I noted the varied examples of that abundant and vigorous race of *indús* [Hindus]. I reflected on what extremes of population that country of two hundred fifty million inhabitants could have attained if, by shaking off its heavy yoke and its misery, it had been able to counteract the periodic famines and endemic plagues thanks to which entire peoples and beings isolated by hundred of miles have paid tribute to death.

The four hundred million Buddhists recruited their greatest contingent of followers in Hindustan.

I recalled the Buddha inside the vitrine, bloated and massive, displaying its huge, naked navel. It's a symbolic navel: the knot that encapsulates the life of the wretched human to be brought into existence. As I left the temple the poor Sinhalese pointed out the navel reverently and with religious respect and spoke to me about the Buddha's mysterious incarnation and purity. His discourse expressed with less eloquence what that fecund land pregnant with abundant vegetation, cradle of all seeds, conveyed to my senses.

When we boarded the ship again, a multitude of launches and rough-hewn pirogues were dancing on the sea along the sides of the ship.

—He! Ahoy! Peseta into the sea! Into the sea!

The diversion was identical to what we saw in Aden. Boys representing the diversity of the Hindu race moistened their bronzed skin, their yellow skin, their reddish skin, their skin of an undefined mixture of colors, plunging and diving in the sea. One group, the most numerous one, stood up at times, and upright in the long, pirogue intoned a slow song from the *Folies Bergère*,[8] accompanied by the repeated thumping of their bent arms against their wet, naked bodies with a rhythmic agility and speed that, rather than movements of their arms, resembled the tremulous beatings of wings.

In the afternoon the ship began to stir and with a gentle movement we sailed toward the mouth of the port. When we approached a French transatlantic ship that was transporting troops to Tonkin,[9] the passengers and crew of both vessels broke out in thunderous *vivas*, saluting each other with caps and handkerchiefs. Very soon the entrance to the port was nothing but a small dot viewed from the stern as we rounded the Punta de Gales.

On the coastline the gigantic peak of Adán[10] was vanishing in the dimness of the fading twilight on the opposite side of the ship.

We were entering the Bay of Bengal. The bell rang for dinner. The lights were on when we reached the deck. The passengers, who had shaken off their hatreds and harshness on land, resumed the habitual relaxed intercourse that they enjoyed during days when they were in good humor. They exchanged impressions of their different excursions and, looking pleased in the midst of the serene evening, they happily breathed the salty air saturated with strong emanations of tar and pitch. These were the same emanations that came from the recesses of the vessel, which in hours of boredom made us irascible and nervous.

At that time, I invariably sat on my ledge with a copy of Macaulay's historical studies. My favorite essay was on Lord Clive.[11]

Looking at the thick veil of shadows that flooded the Bay of Bengal, I reviewed in my imagination all the beautiful pages describing the titanic conquistador of India: *bob* as a child, astounding his parents with his bellicose games; later the insignificant little employee of the English company provoking a duel in terrible circumstances in order to draw attention to his family name. Later on came his audacious undertakings, his joining the army. And finally, the military gifts that in his first martial engagements proved to be harbingers of his exceptional talent, brought him the credit and fame needed to develop his faculties and employ his fortune in the task of ending altogether French dominion in Pondicherry, and to conquer India.

Lord Clive, a man of the stature of Hernán Cortés and Pizarro,[12] gave his country an immense continent. Then, when he was resting on his laurels and savoring his glory—old and ailing, his strength declining—the blackest ingratitude raised public opinion against him. He suffered the horrible fate of ending his days hated by his countrymen who later, in a mood of repentance, tried to amend the injustice, but Death, more pious than men, had already taken possession of the hero's remains. Miserable human inconstancy!

The breeze from land blew across the prow and the rigging vibrated melodiously as the ship moved forward under the mantle of shadows. The passengers, in contrast with recent days, chatted contentedly and in a happy mood threatened to stay up until very late.

The days and nights passed without incident.

One afternoon, many hours after losing the brownish spot of the Nicobar Islands[13] from view, an unexpected happening filled the passengers with emotion and alarm.

The ship was quickly losing speed and shortly stopped altogether.

Someone who was searching the horizon from the deck pointed out a black spot on the sea's smooth surface.

—Men overboard! Men overboard!— Emotions intensified, causing the passengers to move to one side of the vessel. That was the explanation for the sudden stop and, aided by their binoculars, they tried to ascertain how many people had survived the horrible accident—survivors of the eternal drama that depicts the horrible misfortune of a handful of human beings holding on tensely to a pile of boards in the empty ocean.

Despite the unusual movements of the crew we did not see anyone tending to the lifeboats or undertaking any maneuver preliminary to a recovery operation.

—What are they doing?—the most impatient and anxious passengers asked.

The purser, aware of our need to know what was happening, approached us to allay our fears. Smilingly, he disabused us of our momentary illusion.

There were no shipwrecked survivors. That black spot was a tangle of wood and brush torn away from the coast. One man's imagination and the suggestibility of everyone else created the drama. The ship had stopped because of a problem with a screw in one of the piston rods of the ship's engine.

The heat, without the breeze caused by the ship's movement, became intolerable under the sun reflected in the water and pouring fire from above. We were happy to take refuge under the canvas overhangs, laughing heartily at our fantastic impressionability.

NOTES

1. Socotora [Socotra] was made a British protectorate in 1886, the Maldives in 1887.

2. Sinhala was the Sanskrit name for the island. Trapobana was the island's name known to the ancient Greeks. Ceylon is modern Sri Lanka, a British Crown Colony from 1802–1948

3. Malabar, the area of Southern India between Western Ghats and the Arabian Sea.

4. Burguete's use of the word "caste" refers to ethnic groups rather than to castes in the sense of the hereditary social divisions of Hindu society. *Vedda* normally refers to a minority religious group living in Sri Lanka before the arrival of the Sinhalese from North India. *Malays* were inhabitants of modern Malaysia and Indonesia. What he means by *"indio"* is unclear. Here, it seems to mean inhabitants originally from India but without definite tribal affiliations. Like many Spaniards who were in the Philippines for whatever reason during this period, he uses *indio* to describe the people inhabiting the Archipelago who were not Chinese or negritos, that is, the groups he was familiar with.

5. For plants mentioned here and elsewhere in the memoir, see Manuel Blanco, with Pedro G. Galende, *Flora in the Philippines* (Manila: San Augustín Convent, 1993).

6. Pali, a Prakit language native to the Indian subcontinent, was used in earliest extant works of Buddhism and Hinduism. "Mahawanso," is a book on the history of Sri Lanka from the sixth century BCE to 304 CE.

7. The *bil* (*bhil*), *kol,* and the *gond* are some of the ancient tribal populations of India. The *koku* (*korku*) is a tribe of central India and the *puliah* (pulaya) is a Hindu community in South India. See n4 above for the *vedda*.

8. The Folies Bergère, a Parisian music hall at the height of its popularity from the 1800s to the 1920s.

9. From 1886–1896, the French Empire sought to pacify Tonkin (modern-day North Viet Nam). The goal was to establish a French protectorate in Tonkin and to suppress Vietnamese opposition to French rule.

10. Adan is a 7359 foot high mountain in central Sri Lanka. A footprint at the top of the peak was thought by Buddhists to be that of Buddha, by Hindus to be that of Lord Shiva, and by Christians to be that of Adam.

11. Thomas Babington Macaulay (1800–1859), British historian and Whig. In his essay on Robert Clive (1725–1774), Macaulay did not represent Clive as a man free of serious faults but considered him nonetheless the founder of British power in India—power exerted in the service of a great "civilizing" mission (Macaulay, "Lord Clive," in *Critical and Historical Essays*, Volume 1 [first published 1843; Project Gutenberg 2016]. http://www.gutenberg.org/ebooks/2332).

12. Hernán Cortés (1485–1547) was a Spanish conquistador who brought about the fall of the Aztec Empire. Francisco Pizarro (?–1541)was the Spanish conquistador whose expedition conquered the Inca Empire.

13. Denmark sold the Andaman and Nicobar Islands to Britain in 1868. In 1869, they became part of British India. When British Rule in India ended in 1947, they became an Indian Union Territory.

Chapter Five

When the night was well advanced we traversed the narrow Strait of Malacca. Mount Ophir[1] stood out dimly in the shadowy, sepia background. The red lighthouse beam glowed and winked its blood red pupil over the water. A light raced along the coast in the midst of the darkness. We were barely able to distinguish the lights of Malacca in the luminous mist.

On the innumerable reefs and islets to the right, a multitude of beams winked at intervals in the darkness like fearful lookouts scrutinizing the darkness.

We had to wait until daybreak to enter Singapore.[2] We entered the narrow canal covered with lush vegetation that provides access to the town. There were many chalets and villages on the outskirts of the town as was characteristic of all English possessions. The chalets built on either side of the canal were on grounds so enchanting that the magician muse of fairy tales could not have placed as many delightful dwellings there.

I didn't go down to the wharf when the ship docked because we were not going to be there for long. I contented myself with looking from a distance at the beautiful buildings and trim gardens of the European city, and beyond it the extensive indigenous district.

All along the blackish, dirty wharf a long line of steamers were taking on coal as we were. I put up with the dirtiness of the operation and for a long time I stood at one of the railings contemplating a swarm of loathsome, yellow Chinese who, like myriads of ants, carried baskets of coal up the ramps that provided access from the wharf to the ships.

The repugnant appearance of the workers, stained with their natural yellow and with black grime, complemented the poverty evident in their baggy, ragged clothing. Amid the incessant coming and going of the baskets that crushed the pigtails hanging down their backs, a nasal, querulous chattering that went beyond a lament and sounded like a complaint, mixed with the more distant complaints of the vessels' wooden sides lined with surface cracks as they rubbed against the fixed bumpers on the docks. A group of arrogant Sepoys,[3] crossed the wharf and climbed onto the deck of an enormous, big-bellied English steamship.

The commerce of all the strong nations of Europe had many representatives in that vast commercial port. For several hours we took our place among multiple flags from the strong and entrepreneurial countries.

Beyond the city, the coast spread out in a gentle slope toward the east. Everywhere within sight, immense, deep forests stretched to the confines of the north. Deep within these thick and very extensive forests lived the Burmese and the wild tribes of the interior who, when they tired of hunting the beasts that infested the hills and plains, ventured out to mount bloody raids which the dominant English punished with harsh, implacable measures.

We left the port in the afternoon, headed for the outlet to the China Sea. The "Alfonso XIII" passed very close to the Russian squadron as it was saluting the plaza with its powerful cannons.

I looked back at the distant wharf. Above the innumerable masts visible in the port, many flags of all the nations of Europe were floating in the wind. Our flag was furled in the stern and, in its solitary humility, abandoned for the moment by the breeze, it wasn't long before it was lowered. As it folded, it fell onto the deck and there it pulsated like the fluttering wings of a dying bird. Sadly, my thoughts associated this sight with the memory of the bloodletting our fatherland suffered in Cuba and which had just received a new wound on the flank of its Eastern Indies. My mind evoked the entire century of our interior and exterior dismantling. The greatness of Britain reminded me throughout the voyage of our past greatness. The splendor and commercial power of all the nations exaggerated our misery and weakness. The sharp swords of our immortal conquistadors traversed those seas as well as all others, and in each one of their voyages they cut off pieces of extensive, mature kingdoms for the mother country. But the work of conquest amounted to the simple effort of arms while the industry and commerce of our brothers was put aside, fomenting distrust. No capital was invested in the Indies. It was enough to send the blood of needy adventurers, and these men came to number as many as those that greed and hunger caused to surge up from the barren, abandoned native soil.

It didn't take long for the consequences of that disastrous system to be felt. When the fatherland tried to remedy its internal problems, the territory of the colonies, fertilized with the abundant blood of adventurers and conquistadors, felt their abandonment by the metropolis and registered, as well, the vigorous beginnings of European commerce. The colonies noted our poverty and that encouraged a handful of heirs, inheritors of the adventurers of an earlier epoch, to raise the cry of Independence with all the ardor contained in the residue of their veins by three centuries of conquests, violence and adventurers. It was too late, far too late to conquer anew those forgotten territories with the work of commerce that leads to progress. Exhausted by the last efforts of men sent out by the nation, Spain lost the most extensive colonial empire the world had ever seen. Meanwhile, other countries with a modest work of conquest, seconded by the commerce and industry of their fellow countrymen, were acquiring extensive markets, not by exchanging blood for gold, but rather by economizing both products and extending the conquest with the careful and untiring task of work and common effort.

In both Indies we had only two markets left from our immense colonial dominion and at almost the same time the two rose up in rebellion. We had to make an effort to subjugate them both. So ships and more ships went off filled with troops recruited in conditions of misery and, with patriotic sentiment lulled by continuous internal fights, the men barely comprehended the life and death commercial problem that they were meant to resolve.

The port disappeared in the distance, and distance swallowed the colors and forms of the multiple foreign flags and innumerable masts.

When we had traveled a few miles, the bell on the bridge announced a ship sighting and very soon the news spread that the ship approaching us at the prow at a majestic pace was the "Colón," which belonged to the same company as ours, and was the one I took when I returned from Cuba.

The crew was happy. Salutation flags and signal flares were prepared. The passengers on their feet, vibrant and excited, awaited the arrival of their fellow patriots who were returning to the beloved land where all of us had left loved ones.

Finally, after a voyage of twenty-six days, we saw the red and yellow flag waving on another ship. Our two ships passed very close together amidst the hoarse salutes of their powerful sirens, the bursting of the flares, and the waving of flags and pennants.

Standing on their chairs to see better, the faces of the passengers revealed anxiety and emotion. On the deck of the "Colón" many soldiers dressed in striped uniforms saluted us waving their straw hats.

A hoarse groan from a siren split the air and was followed by a weak and tremulous "Long live Spain," that drifted across the water. A delirious explosion burst out on the "Alfonso XIII," and in between voices shouting *vivas* that were struggling against tears, an enthusiastic salvo of applause greeted the sick, the wounded, and the invalids whom war was returning to the bosom of the country and to their loving mothers.

When the "Colón" vanished from the horizon in the smoke it left behind, the flag, after waving with an exhausted effort, was lowered onto the deck resembling, as it fell, the beating of the palpitating wings of a dying bird.

The crossing of the China Sea during the next few days was very difficult, so rough that it kept the majority of the passengers confined to their cabins.

At sunset on the fourth day, we saw the coastline of Luzón and the elevated range of Mariveles was the first land we spied on the Magellanic archipelago.

The sea apparently withdrew its stormy defiance from its surface waters, but preserving its rancor deep below, it allowed that rancor to be felt at times with what sailors call the "sea within."

The joy of seeing the coast and ending the journey emboldened even the shakiest passengers. They began to invade the deck with faces the color of green seaweed.

The sun was setting at the stern in lovely shades of crimson and red when we traversed the only viable canal between the small island of Corregidor and Luzón that permits entry to Manila Bay.

We left the port of Mariveles on the left and rounding a rocky promontory we entered fully into the large bay whose size makes it seem like a gulf.

Seen from the port side of the ship the deep inlet of Bulacán and Pampanga extends beyond the horizon. On the opposite side, the range of the Sungay was descending in gradual slopes to the distant and irregular coast. That is where Bacoor, Cavite, Imus, Noveleta are situated—the theatre of the most recent actions that, according to our information, was in the power of the insurrectionists.

In the distance, from the prow we could distinguish a confused line of mountains and coasts.

Night had fallen when we reached the place to drop anchor. And in sight of Manila whose small lights twinkled over a large space like scattered, dying embers, the "Alfonso XIII" cut its engine, and we were left stealthily awaiting daylight.

NOTES

1. Mount Ophir is a 4,186-foot-high mountain in Malaysia. For antiquarian Christian travelers, it evoked the land (Ophir) mentioned in the Torah or Tanakh.

2. Singapore was a British possession beginning in 1824. In 1826, it was placed under the jurisdiction of British India and remained so when Burguete saw it in 1896.

3. After 1857, an Indian soldier serving in the British Indian Army was known as a Sepoy.

Chapter Six

I lodged in the Hotel de Oriente, situated in Tondo,[1] the early name for Manila, and today one of the most extensive districts in the city.

I was given a large room on the ground floor at the end of a long, wide hallway paved with rich, magnificent wooden floors.

In the center of the spacious room, which had more furniture than was needed, there was a bed, lost under a double, closely woven mosquito net.

A third pillow that was as long as the bed occupied the place where a body might lie. Naturally, it caught my attention. The *bata* [an *indio* manservant] in reply to my question explained that it was there for the sleeper to embrace through the night. Strange custom and an extraordinary notion!

Shaking off the indolence caused by the sea journey and with growing impatience, I changed clothes and went out determined to make my official presentations that same day.

I walked along the wide plaza on which the hotel was situated seeking relief on the shady side of the street from the burning embrace of the sun that in a sky of purest blue heated the luminous atmosphere with the hot breath of a forge.

Slow moving, sleepy carabaos, necks bent under the weight of their enormous horns, pulled big carts and, driven by *indios*, constituted the traffic along the street that led to the road to the port.

I came upon an infinity of *indios* of both sexes who struck me as a single pair repeated over and over again. The men were dressed in starched shirts worn outside their pants, which left their legs and feet bare from the knee down. They covered their heads with straw hats or colorful headscarves. Men who did not cover their heads displayed a tangle of hair so thick and curly that it was enough to protect their heads and almost explained the reason for the less than medium height of those men with heads flattened in the back, prominent cheekbones and snub noses. Below the dark stain of hair that grew down over their foreheads it was difficult to discern the wan, muddy tone of their skin and even their features.

The women, wearing transparent, light blouses that left one shoulder exposed, walked along shod in colored or black sandals with wooden soles. They let their beautiful hair fall loose down their backs, and the graceful movement of their arms—not without charm—caused their hips to sway rhythmically. Their stiff and dark outer skirts, tight at the waist and ending at their knees, veiled what modesty demands must be concealed, leaving their legs visible under the flimsy cloth of their petticoats.

With their identical physiognomies, only the sweetness and softness of the women's slanted eyes made it possible to distinguish between the faces of both sexes.

I crossed through the Chinese quarter next to the plaza. Along the principal street and behind the colonnades that extended in rows on either side, I saw many Chinese with yellow faces and sickly appearances smoking opium, sitting indolently at the doors of gloomy hovels and wretched stores filled with customers. Or they were chewing *buyo* [betel nut, betel leaf and lime]. I had already seen *buyo* on the mouths of male and female *indios*. It stained their lips and gums a bright red that made their faces resemble clowns, or it gave them a look of cannibalistic ferocity.[2] I left the Chinese quarter with its pungent, spicy smells, and rounded the plaza that led to the Escolta.

European commerce was located along the street with this name, occupying the ground floors of tall, grand buildings.

At that hour there were so many customers walking through the streets as well as landaus, carts, *quilers*[3] and all kinds of coaches circulating along the street heading for the turn to the bridge, that walking there was impossible and I had to hire a landau to take me to the walled city.

The entrance to the Bridge of Spain, a magnificent construction of stone and iron, constituted a large space inundated with light, under a very fine cloud of dust that sparkled in the sun which was pouring out its burning fire. On each side of the buttresses at the entrance a veteran pair of the guard—*indios* of a robust stature, grave and circumspect under their felt helmets and proud in the blue uniforms that left their legs and feet bare—demanded rigorous observation of the rule for taking turns in the queue for the entrance and exit of carriages.

We crossed the bridge. Along the length of the sidewalk with railings on either side, a multitude of people dressed in bright and loud colors came and went: male and female *indios*, soldiers from Spain, indigenous soldiers, male and female *mestizos*[4] dressed in white drill of a dazzling stiffness like that of employees on the Peninsula. Carriages noisily marking their passage in the center of the road carried the laziest or the most diligent passengers. The Pasig River flowed gently beneath our feet and upon its waters ran the small steamboats with unobstructed decks that cross the river, or convoys of enormous launches with canvas coverings and rails made of reeds slipped along slowly, replete with merchandise and sunken under its stacked up weight. On the right, docks had been built on the river's broad banks. A multitude of boats of lesser tonnage were tied up there, submerging their gray swollen bellies in the water, creating a kind of dance at the docks consisting of a swarm of ropes and riggings from which hung canvas, flags, waxed banners and pennants ablaze in the sun or agitated by the breeze as it blew in from the nearby outlet of the port.

On the left, beyond the shade that the bridge threw over the water, the river glittered in the sun's rays. It narrowed as it left the hanging bridge that I saw on the left and disappeared in a bend, taking with it its banks festooned with gigantic plumes of greenery and splashed with innumerable chalets that amongst branches of foliage hid their enchanting, marvelous architecture.

Ahead lay a radial system of avenues covered with shade and set between rows of leafy trees. It served as a beltway for the walled city that lay beyond at the end of a slope, and which lifted into space the towers and ridges of its tall buildings, poorly guarded by the low and shady bastion walls that dripped humidity and mossy lichen amid the dry and luminous atmosphere of that diaphanous and serene midday.

Crossing a drawbridge, we entered through one of the doors whose gate was secured by an indigenous guard.

Most of the buildings in the old city are made of stone and its houses, placed in straight lines, are traced in accord with the plan of its immortal founder Legazpi.[5]

There is less activity here than in the outskirts of the city. My coach moved along the uneven stones of the roadway fronting numerous superb, elegant convents. The few pedestrians inhabiting the old city traversed streets that invariably leave one sidewalk in the shade. Among the people on the street are pairs of friars of all the communities, Augustinians, Order of Augustinian Recollects, Capuchins, Dominicans, under their white, brownish or black habits.[6] Dragging their sandaled feet lazily along the sidewalks, they speak in low voices and walk slowly in time with the clicking sound of the beads on their long rosaries.

Sudden gusts of wind reach the high part of the city that looks out to the sea and blowing through the streets, saturates them with a delicious, humid freshness. An incessant pealing of bells envelopes old Manila with impressive, penetrating sound. Within the circle of its lichen-covered walls the city sleeps through the absence or the laziness of its inhabitants, bathed in the light and burning sun at the top of its tall buildings and moistened in the shade, its multiple short streets immersed in sepulchral silence.

The coach rolls along disturbing the august peace, the cloister-like serenity anointed with mystery and shadow that envelopes a city whose silence is interrupted at times by the footfalls of the few transients, the sounds of doors shutting, the slow pacing of the city patrols, or the soft and muted contact of the missionaries' sandals on the sidewalks.

We arrived at the plaza of the Cathedral,[7] a magnificent temple built in 1879, grave and severe, in the Byzantine style, concocted in accord with the impurities of modern taste. It is one of the façades on a quadrangular plaza, improvised on a small parterre. The Captain-General's building is located on one of the corners of the square.

Inside and out, the building exudes an artificial refinement and rococo majesty. An entrance guard, fully armed and bearing a halberd, was positioning a pair of guards on the first steps of the monumental stairway that, like the ceiling's wooden coffering, conveys majesty with what little remains of its theatricality.

Once I had completed my mission of making courtesy calls and confirming my military duties, I returned to the city beyond the walls and paused to rest in the tobacco shop on Escolta Street.

I received affectionate greetings from innumerable shipmates and warm embraces from comrades in my old company or from college before I was able to find a place at one of the fully occupied tables. Men from the Peninsula gathered there and the only talk was of the war and the latest events. Officers convalescing from their wounds on crutches or with their arms in slings, recounted the horrors they experienced in the hospitals or provided interesting details of the most recent actions. Driven crazy by their stories and by the dense tobacco smoke, I left, after drinking a glass of gin, determined to return to the inn where lunch was doubtless ready.

I crossed Escolta Street in the midst of a tangle of carriages and the press of pedestrians. I entered the Chinese Quarter whose proprietors still stood imperturbably in the doorways smoking slender pipes that infected the air which, heated by the sun, made me feel unhinged. I headed for the plaza avoiding the coaches that went by in a hurry and the slow moving carriages drawn by sleepy big-horned carabaos following the drivers who were contentedly chewing the *buyo* that stained their lips red and lent their flattened faces a sinister appearance.

The dining room of the hotel was located on the ground floor, covered by a canopy. A small hallway adorned with attractive flowerpots formed the entrance. The dining room was a square patio. In the back the proprietress sat behind a counter, performing the duties of a *maitre d'*, seeing to it that the *indios* served the many tables according to a rigorous rule of precedence. The plants in the entranceway lined up by the door, along with the canopy, contributed to the impression of a delicious freshness.

I took a table together with several companions and waited for the *indios* who, barefooted and diligent, ran across the tiled floor, solicitous to everyone and attentive to themselves. With their embroidered or plain, impeccably ironed shirts outside their pants, they hastened to attend to all the customers' needs and served them rather whimsically with confused gestures, not exempt from deceit and laziness. Very near us, a couple from the Peninsula occupied the end of a table. I found out from companions who had been there for some time that the husband was a provincial governor who, having made a decent fortune was waiting for the occasion to return to Spain with his . . . (Here, malice put the sacrament in quarantine).

His gracious companion sported two very expensive earrings in perfect accord with the notable beauty of their owner. Between remarks made during the indifferent and good natured conversation she carried on with her companion, she discreetly scrutinized each one of the newly arrived guests, certain of drawing new admiring glances from the numerous male company who moved about in their seats, changing positions in an attempt to satisfy their avid glances when the numerous servants momentarily blocked their view of the woman.

Certain of the impression she was making, she sat up straight, her slender bust close to the edge of the table and, breathless with the intoxication of female vanity that colored the glowing cheeks of her face, framed in a tangle of golden curls, she lowered her eyelids the better to conceal her discreet glances, and at their tremulous fluttering she pretended to pay attention to her companion with absorbed attention and admiring modesty.

When lunch—spent in long commentaries on the war—was over, I returned to my room, disposed to write several letters and to enter notes on the journey in my diary.

In mid afternoon I was surprised in the midst of these tasks by the unexpected visit of a childhood friend who had been employed for several years in the Philippines and who, learning of my arrival, came to embrace me with heartfelt affection and to offer me his coach and his knowledge of the place in order to visit the outskirts of Manila.

I put away my notes and after handing my keys to the *bata* we headed down the wide hallway at the end of which an unexpected emotion left us breathless and amazed . . . Because the door had been indiscreetly left ajar, it revealed a long mirror in which the white and luminous bust of the ex governor's companion was reflected, nude from the waist up, displaying the earrings in her small ears half hidden amongst blond locks of curly hair. Her towel fell in multiple folds, dropping to her feet in a whitish and disordered confusion of towels and foam in the adjacent bathtub covered with floating sponges. The amiable young woman supported herself on the edge of the bed facing the mirror, her fragile, small breasts open to the air. Her rosy nipples were of a color more intense than that left by the traces of the scrub brush which the maid had carefully drawn along her smooth, moist skin . . .

A slight cry followed by a door being slammed and by harsh words directed at the maid, accompanied us to the coach that was waiting at the door. We got in and, rounding the Tondo Bridge began our excursion.

It was all of an endless beauty and so varied that I can scarcely recall today all the magnificent examples of light, color and form. We traversed the Iris Road: the vicinity of the Binondo quarter, the Paco Road and a succession of broad avenues planted with gigantic trees that half concealed dappled, small gardens, and served as jealous guardians of attractive houses of bamboo and *nipa palm*, set among palm trees, feathery leaves of wild cane and tangles of old banana plants.

Moving along with the strong gusts of air caused by the spirited pair that was drawing the coach, we passed before beautiful and varied edifices of oriental artifice and taste inspired by the giddiness of fantasy or by realities plucked from the black magic of a vague fairy tale.

Tropical flora burst forth in infinite variety.

We crossed street after street of an original and varied beauty.

The sun was setting in the west and at the humid kiss of approaching nightfall the *ilang-ilang*, the *sampaga*, the *calechuchi*, the *sabiqui*, the *pasionaria* and an infinity of aromatic plants burned by the sun and thirsty for dew opened their pores.

At twilight's delightful onset we entered the perfumed avenue of Malacanang. The interlaced leaves of trees meeting overhead from either side of the street revealed fragments of the salmon-colored sky in the West. The sumptuous and elegant properties on the left and right of the road rose up on their bamboo columns and allowed us in passing to see through their open windows by the light of Venetian lanterns or enormous globes of blue or red crystal all of the discreet wealth of its rooms. They were decorated according to Japanese taste, whose agreeable and playful style harmonized with the capricious and picturesque groupings of *lomboys, guayabos, naranjos, cajeles* and *guanabanos* which among tufts of slender palms and the narrow leaves of bamboo swaying, not without complaint, in the breeze, decorated the ground and the dividing walls covered with a very fine, green moss interwoven with multicolored leaves.

Night fell and the tilbury's lanterns were lit. It rolled swiftly along the areas lighted by voltaic arcs that appeared here and there. The vigorous pair, thanks to the breeze, blew the white foam that covered their harnesses toward us and carried us in a dizzying run toward the broad roadway that leads to the Paseo de la Luneta.

Shortly, we came to the Malecon and took our place in the long line of coaches whose lights, forming a pleasing curve in the distance, were entering the parallel line of coaches returning from the drive.

That was the obligatory ride and return of coaches along the length of the plaza, licked by the waves, before entering the road to the Luneta.

When it was our turn I was able to examine at leisure that unique and obligatory roadway in which there was a kiosk for daily musical performances. Nearby, on an elevated, sandy rise, from six to eight in the evening, people strolled past a row of chairs.

At that time of the evening there were few friars who, stretched out in their coaches wearing white habits and circlets, were easy to confuse at a distance with the white, vaporous garb of the ladies.

The ladies, with their heads uncovered, passed by reclining indolently in their carriages. They greeted the groups occupying the chairs with slight inclinations of their heads and discreet gestures.

On the side of the drive close to the Malecon, I got down from the coach to take some refreshment with my friend at a place with tables in the open air, lit with small lanterns that lent it the appearance of a fair.

Shortly afterwards, we joined the strollers where black and white suits dotted the diverse groups with their numerous uniforms.[8]

People talked about the war; young people of both sexes chatted amusingly and exchanged amorous glances. They all killed time in the midst of the very fine dust raised by our feet along with the breeze heavy with humidity which came from the sounding, darkened sea, which was lit in the East by the multiple lights of ships anchored in the port and in the West by its distant lights and bonfires in enemy territory.

We returned to the hotel. The Bridge of Spain opened at night under the stream of harsh light cast by the voltaic arcs.

The walled city barely revealed the indistinct shapes of its buildings in the gloaming. To the right and left of the river the glowing lights of the villages and the boats floated in the dense shadows, accompanied by the sound of the murmuring, measured, lapping of the water.

I dined with my friend, recalling the beautiful sights of our excursion. The same couple we observed at luncheon took their place in a corner. I thought I detected a note of angry severity in the blonde's blue eyes as she passed her discreet and vain glances around the dining room.

Tired from the day's activities, I said good night to my friend following a long after dinner chat and retired to my room, determined to go to bed.

Stretched out on the bed, I heard the voice of the ex governor's companion in the hallway ordering a coach.

I closed my eyes to the adventure of the afternoon and with a sudden burst of anger threw the third pillow to the floor, thinking it a strange whim, a quirky, useless object.

NOTES

1. Manila derives from Tagalog *Maynila*. During Burguete's residence in the Archipelago, Tondo was a province and a district in the city of Manila. John Foreman described the Hotel de Oriente: it "opened in Binondo in January 1889, in a large two-storeyed building, with 83 rooms for the public service and stabling 25 horses. It was the first building specially erected in the colony for an hotel. The accommodation and board were good. It ranked with the best hotels in the East" (Foreman, *The Philippine Islands* (1905), 3rd ed. [London: T. Fisher Unwin, 1906; Project Gutenberg 2007], 352, http://www.gutenberg.org/ebooks/22815).

2. Foreman's description: "To the newly-arrived European, it is very displeasing to have to converse with a native betel-eater whose teeth and lips appear to be smeared with blood" (*Philippine Islands*, 304).

3. In Carlos Ría-baja's *El Desastre Filipino: Memorias de un prisionero* (Barcelona: Tipografía de la Académica de Serra Hermanos y Russell, 1899), 164, refers to *quiles*—not *quilers*—rather vaguely as "a special vehicle of the country."

4. The *mestizos* referred to in this passage were probably of *indio* [indigenous] and Spanish ancestry. More numerous were the *mestizos de sangley*, of Chinese and *indio* background. Burguete does not mention the latter. His description of the Chinese he observed in the Chinese quarter later in this chapter appears to refer only to Chinese who are not of mixed Chinese and *indio* ancestry. See the Introduction to this translation for a discussion of these terms.

5. Miguel Lopez de Legazpi (c.1510–1572) was a Spanish explorer who set out with orders from Philip II to colonize the Philippines. In 1571, he founded the city of Manila.

6. For friars and their role in the Philippines at about the time of Burguete's presence there, it is useful to start with his contemporary, Marcelo H. Del Pilar whose *Monastic Supremacy in the Philippines*, translated from the Spanish by Encarnación Alzona (Quezón City: Philippine Historical Association, 1958), opposed the continued presence of the friars in the Philippines. See also John N. Schumacher, S.J., *Revolutionary Clergy. The Filipino Clergy and the Nationalist Movement, 1850–1903* (Quezon City: Ateneo de Manila University Press, 1981).

7. The Cathedral Burguete described was in its seventh incarnation. Earthquakes destroyed the preceding structures, and in 1880 the bell tower was toppled by another earthquake.

8. Spanish soldiers wore black and white suits for daily use.

Chapter Seven

On the days that followed, my habits conformed to an hourly schedule, and that schedule was what was customary in the colony inhabited by Spaniards from the Peninsula.

The Katipunan[1] was the most common topic of conversation. I became aware of the sinister, hair-raising details of that vast conspiracy that failed in the lodges, then fled to the countryside, and in the dry terrain of old hatreds and thorny overgrowths of anger was beginning to catch fire with war's devastating flame.

The voracious fire had invaded almost all the provinces and it threatened to consume all the territory of Luzón.

The last operations in Imus and Noveleta,[2] where the insurrectionists attempted to invade the province of Cavite by sea, was disastrous for our arms. The consequences were so serious that if the disaster were not remedied right away, the frequent desertions of the indigenous troops would leave the regiments nearly devoid of soldiers.

The Katipunesque conspiracy still horrified the witnesses who escaped, thanks to the miraculous denunciation of the plot by an old woman.

Even minor accidents on the street struck fear in those present. The friars always travelled in pairs armed with heavy canes. The Peninsular element that did not form part of the guerrillas or of the battalions of volunteers, made the revolver an inseparable part of their trousers.

One morning, in the Escolta, they began to tell me about the plot and I agreed to join them in their usual afternoon stroll to see some of the sites of the action.

Mortal risks, miraculously avoided, provided all the vagueness of fantasy in the imaginations of my narrators. A fantastic tension caused by simple recollections fed the narration with dark, horrendous details, whose essential, colorless reality sufficed to create fear in one's spirit.

The sinister Katipunan conspiracy recruited followers in the indigenous population with no distinction of age or sex. A simple incision in the arm was enough for those fanatics to seal their oath with blood, and those who joined the conspiracy believed from that moment on that they were freed from ties of what should have been unlimited gratitude, and even from blood ties. The sacred fire of independence would purify the greatest crimes and would serve in future to fuse affection, gratitude, love—old precepts that in the view of the sect's members would serve to solder the links of the former chain of slavery.

My narrators found examples of all the horrible, inhumane acts perpetrated by the beast in man, concrete examples of behavior distorted by the instinct for liberty: an *indio* who had served in the same house from childhood, after enjoying the prosperity of his masters for many years, swore that he would exterminate the family once he had taken the oath. Or it was a youngster who became a man with the help of a peninsular Spaniard and who, as a result of favors and indulgences, felt a filial affection for his master not unlike that characteristic of blood ties. A mother sought an occasion to avenge herself on the progenitor of her offspring. No one could escape the demands of the Katipunan and perhaps no one would escape the horrible massacre of peninsular Spaniards scheduled for a given day. Men, women, children, all would have succumbed to the dagger, poison or mob violence spurred on by the power of a race that counted its adherents by the thousands and by means of a simple incision purged the body of the most intimate ties of affection.

In the afternoon our coach crossed the Bilibid road en route to the Paco road. The horrors my companions related, accompanied by facial expressions and gestures, were lost in the cloud of dust that the landau passed through in the midst of the calm and sweet serenity of the afternoon. The sun, tinged with crimson and shades of oriental dried meat, was setting in the West amidst small, rose-colored lacy clouds. The air was saturated with the aroma of *ilang ilang* and *sampango*.

I saw a multitude of male and female *indios* walking on the streets or standing at the doors of their dwellings. They were of slight build and their postures revealed humble attitudes. Beneath the curly tangle of their hair and the multicolored clothes they wore, they looked at me with a good natured and respectful mien.

Was it true that among those people of kindly and humble aspect and under that sky of a languid and voluptuous blue it was possible to plan such horrors?

In response, my friends pointed out the miserable shantytowns of indigenous people, which, like a sea of dry brush, extended far into the distance,

Chapter Seven

blocking off Manila. That was the principal reinforcement; the reserve army chosen for the assault, not at the instigation of the Katipunan, but rather because of four centuries of misery and hunger that the many pages of the dominant catechism had not been able to sweeten.

The following afternoon I took the train to join my posting in San Fernando de la Pampanga. As we passed through the outlying neighborhoods I looked out the train windows for a long time, contemplating the successive waves of huts made of cane and *nipa* whose ground floor was raised because of the muddy terrain. Those were the neighborhoods that aroused suspicions of disloyalty and fears of strong resistance. The huts were built right up to the railroad tracks and in their windows, which formed a continuous opening on the four sides of the dwellings, families showed themselves with numerous children like multiple flocks of sheep, lifting their naked and chocolate-colored flesh to the winds and the flies.

The misery of the *bajais* [huts] bare of furniture, contrasted with the groups of banana trees, palm trees, and plentiful, colorful vegetation serving as a belt around those miserable huts that resembled dwellings built over water. They were scattered along the railway track, separated from each other by patches of land sown with betel and cordoned off by stakes.

We began to traverse the immense, arid plains that took on a yellowish color due to the dry stalks of *palai* [rice], recently cut down to the ground.

On our right the hills of San Mateo rose up and, before us, dotting the immense plain, feathery cane fields formed capricious *bosquetos* [groves] or winding lines that were lost in the confines of the yellow plain.

In every station the detachment charged with protecting the friendly town and exercising vigilance over the railroad, formed on the platform at our arrival.

Above the groups of huts in the towns we passed, the indispensable convent rose up magnificently and next to it the great tower of the church that rang out its bells or remained mute and silent, overcome by the solemn torpor of the vast plain.

At one stop shortly before crossing the great river of the Pampanga a unit boarded our train that was separated from the column operating at that time in San Miguel de Mayumo.

I was able to observe that the soldiers, although they wore clothes stuck to their bodies with the dirt of those dusty plains and sweat baked by the sun during their fatiguing marches, did not present the disastrous and exhausted appearance of soldiers in Cuba.

The river of the Pampanga like a ribbon of burnished steel disappeared in the midst of the arid plains. Like dark points the *vintas*[3] sails stained the shining edges of the water that was narrowing within our view, on its way to the mouth of the river.

The landscape, more pleasant than at the outset, featured more vegetation, and long patches of greenery relieved the aridity of the rice plantings.

At nightfall we were able to make out the immense mass of the Carbello foothills.

Immediately, we passed a *pinac* [lagoon] from which big-footed birds rose up in low and heavy flight. And when the night was very advanced, along an avenue of sturdy, gigantic trees that the locomotive lit up two or three times with the flaming breath of its funnel, I arrived at my destination.

NOTES

1. The Katipunan, organized as a secret society in 1892 and discovered by the Spanish government in 1896, had as its principal objective independence from Spain. Masonry was a primary influence on its ideology and rituals. Accounts differ as to how Spanish authorities became aware of the secret society. According to one version, which was likely to have been the version Ricardo Burguete was familiar with, its existence was discovered in August 1896 when a member of the society, Teodoro Patiño, informed his sister, a nun, of his membership in the society along with its agenda. She passed on the information to Sor Teresa de Jesus who urged Patiño to confess what he knew to Father Mariano Gil. Gil then informed the Spanish authorities of the Society's plans to kill Spaniards and wrest control of the government from the colonizers. See Gregorio F. Zaide, *Documentary History of the Katipunan Discovery: A crítico-historical study of the Betrayal of the KKK. New Revelations*, 2nd ed. (Manila: 1931), 32–58. A few lines below, Burguete remarks on recent actions of the Katipunan conspiracy noting that the "Katipunesque conspiracy still horrified the witnesses who escaped, thanks to the miraculous denunciation of the plot by an old woman." I do not know the specific incident he is referring to here. A contemporary Spanish resident in the Philippines wrote: "Almost all of them [insurrectionist plots] have been uncovered and denounced [to priests] by indigenous women very devoted to Spain" (*Filipinas: Problema fundamental por un español de larga residencia en aquellas islas* [Madrid: Aguado, 1891], 42n2). The power and influence of the friars over devout women was one of the factors that caused the insurrectionists to demand the expulsion of the friars from the Philippines. See Francis St. Clair, *The Katipunan or The Rise and Fall of the Filipino Commune* (Manila; Tip. "Amigos del País, Palacio 258, 1902); Teodoro A. Agoncillo, *Revolt of the Masses: The Story of Bonifacio and the Katipunan* (Quezon City: University of the Philippines, 1956).

2. See chapter 26, n2.

3. A *vinta* is a traditional boat from Mindanao with sails of vertical striped colors.

Chapter Eight

I spent the night in San Fernando de la Pampanga and, after long hours of preparation for the march ahead which robbed me of sleep, I set out the following morning with my company. We formed part of a column charged with operating in the province of Bataan. I was to lead the advance guard and at daybreak I joined the soldiers on the outskirts of the town. We continued along the road to Bacolor, the capital of Pampanga. The entire road runs through neighborhoods [*barangays*] whose lines of houses border the two sides of the road.

Our journey along the dusty road was a triumphal march that made me momentarily forget war operations and believe myself transported to an excursion on horseback.

At the doors and windows of the huts, decorated with flags and pennants, a multitude of *indios* who were dressed in shirts with starched shirt tails, barefooted, and with heads covered with shiny felt hats, burst out as we passed with cries of "*Viva España!*" produced by a swarm of women and children wearing the most garish outfits, suitable for days of festivity.

Loyalty or fear led in equal parts to the excessive howling of *vivas*.

Very close to Bacolor and all along the line of huts, the people and their band of musicians came out to the road to receive us.

The convent bells rang out and the exuberance of the welcome reached its limit in that town of seventeen thousand souls.

In the plaza that features a simple monument to the memory of Anda Salazar,[1] the troops rested and the officers, after saluting the governor who was installed in one of the three buildings constructed of masonry in the town, proceeded to form ranks again in order to continue the march.

We crossed the river Betis on a bridge of wood and cane and continued the day's march to Lubao, accompanied by the musicians and followed by the incessant acclamations of the *indios* all along the clusters of dwellings on the road.

In Lubao the soldiers were lodged in a convent, which served a splendid mess, a gift of the Dominican Fathers.

We officers and the column's staff officers ate in the refectory, handsomely feted by the fathers.

The community had gathered together several tables in the spacious dining room that evoked a cloistral solemnity and was saturated with the scents of sap and shade that the breeze drew from the bushy trees in the patio and carried up to the high windows. The guests were taking their places and shortly afterwards numerous servants, all *indios*, began to ceremoniously remove the plates and wines from an abundant and succulent meal.

The conversation again turned to what was happening in the war. In the view of the good fathers, pacification would be an undertaking lasting only a few months. They counted on winning because of the unreflective nature of the *indios* and their religiosity. They gave us details of the last developments. The insurrection had not dared to set foot in Pampanga because it feared the fidelity and fierceness of its inhabitants, submissive parishioners, fervent, enthusiastic Christians who had begun to adore the insignia of the fatherland as a result of seeing it used as a canopy on the altars of Christ.

The bells of the temple next to us struck solemnly and gravely at the top of the tower and at times their vibrations muffled the uproar of shouts and music that the indigenous multitude offered to celebrate the presence of the soldiers in the plaza.

Gusts of wind carried up to us the note of majestic, calm happiness in the ceremonious, grave roar of a major celebration.

The fathers did not neglect the honors of the table and the conversation, animated by good wines, returned tirelessly to the endless topic of the war.

The only insurrectionist bands that had reached those parts did not dare to cross the river of Pampanga close to Florida-Blanca, the next resting point on our itinerary, according to what I heard from the head of our column.

When the dinner was over, we moved on to take coffee in the salon liberally provided with enormous wooden chairs, genuine ceremonial chairs with long arms on which local custom permitted us to rest our legs.

Late in the afternoon, accompanied with affectionate cordiality by the fathers to the outskirts of the town, we resumed the march along a dusty road that under an avenue of trees created here and there circles of shade.

Our digestion in those hours, robbed of a siesta, slowed down the column's march during the first kilometers of the day's journey. As the sun was going down the breeze began to stir, coming from the far off horizon closed off with forests and tinted on high with scarlet. The wind was raising dust on the road and it refreshed our sweaty bodies as the column passed through copious corn fields, immense cane fields dotted with *trapiches* [primitive sugar mills] followed by small groves of bamboo, in groups alternating with muddy fields in which carabaos, bulls, and much valued mixed race nags, little higher than dogs, grazed.

The column marched forward in the dark as the last reflections of twilight faded away. We pushed on without resting until we saw the lights of Florida-Blanca and passed by the first rows of huts near the town.

NOTE

1. Simón de Anda y Salazar (1709–1776), was the governor of the Philippines from 1770 to 1776. He mustered largely indigenous forces to defeat the British who occupied Manila in 1762. The Spanish government had capitulated to the British, but by 1764 Anda y Salazar had repelled them.

Chapter Nine

I was instructed to lodge my company next to the property that the general had chosen. Its owner reserved rooms for me and for my officers. His name was N . . . He was from the Peninsula and had spent many hard-working years in the country. In the town where he currently lives he had spent enough time, thanks to his diligence and to good luck, to achieve a state of wellbeing that approached splendor.

His house, which was constructed and decorated in the style of the lacustrine chalets in Manila, was a delicious nest that appeared beneath a dark blot of branches. In the dense shadows of the night which the bushy trees in the small plaza in which the house was situated made even thicker, the dazzling, magical house appeared in the artificial, whitish light pouring out of all its open windows. This light contrasted with the colored reflections of the innumerable little lanterns in the Venetian style hanging from the uneven cornice or fastened onto the windows. They formed a capricious garland of multicolored beads twinkling in graduated, gracious curves all along the walls and ended by forming two lines of points of a soft and luminous scarlet that were strung along the slanted balustrades of the principal stairway.

Señor N . . . introduced his four daughters to us. During the day's march my head felt heavy because of the unrelenting sun, and my pupils were so affected by the suddenness of that outpouring of light in the midst of shadows that I was nearly blinded. The daughters of Señor N . . . who were ceremonious and stiff under the white foam of tatting and lace on their dresses, appeared before my eyes like figures in a theatrical apotheosis.

We undertook our march very early the next morning and during the first few hours, I recalled the scenes from the night before: the fantastic appearance of Señor N's daughters who seemed to me to appear amidst clouds of rainbow-colored lights; Señor N . . . with his severe and taciturn look, speaking during the supper and in the conversation afterwards in the garden with a vitality and energy that were beaten down at every turn by discouragement. I reviewed the contrast between that gracious nest decked out splendidly at our arrival, a nice mark of courtesy along with an animated show of delight at our arrival—and the fact that even in that night of fiesta, after complying with all the duties of courtesy toward their guests, they wept over their sorrows between sips of tea in a corner of the garden illuminated by the smiling and festive lights of the strings of multicolored little lanterns.

Señor N . . . for two years a widower, was suffering from a painful cardiac infection, countered up to the present by divine mercy and by the lavish care given him by his daughters. He had no illusions regarding the insurrection. The bitter pessimism of his chronic illness he carried over to contemporary events. The devastation of two of his properties by insurrectionist bands was a cruel blow that revealed to him the coming disaster of his life first, and later his hacienda. He had no illusions. He had been in the country for many years. The insurrection would be formidable and would bleed Spain dry. He would not be a witness to the disaster; he would soon follow his wife, dead and safe at last after a thousand troubles in that ungrateful land. But his daughters without kith and kin, without friends, once Spain was expelled from that fertile colony, would see the despoiling of their properties and the distribution of those lands that the hard work and vigilance of their parents developed. Who knows how far the violence and reprisals of the victors might go?

His daughters in their formal vestments, animated and shaken by the gloomy premonition, tried to instill hope in their father as they had done before.

Day was dawning as we moved forward and shortly after crossing the river, after traversing an extensive cane field, we saw the terrain devastated by the insurrectionist bands' last incursion.

A large sea of ash blown into spirals by the wind covered the terrain where the extensive cane fields had been planted. Those fields of a uniform gray had the sinister drained color that I saw that morning on the face of Señor N . . . He refused to go beyond the boundaries of the town when he came out to say goodbye to the column. He told us that he didn't want to see the horrible devastation of his fields once again. It mattered little to him since, after all, his days were numbered, but he wanted to spare his good daughters any painful emotion.

I recalled the farewell in early dawn at the foot of the peristyle where the night before the four young women appeared before my eyes like images of a radiant theatrical apotheosis. Modest, simple, their hair a tangle of curls unlike the elaborate coiffure of the night before, they came out smiling to bid us goodbye and charged us all with not allowing their poor father to go beyond the town boundaries.

Chapter Nine

The sight of that immense field incinerated by war, the contrast of the finery they wore the night before and the unkempt appearance of the four orphans in the early morning lent force in my mind to the sad premonition of the poor old man.

Who knows whether the day might not be far off in which those animated creatures would have to clothe their absolute orphan-hood in miserable rags!

Beyond the plain we saw blotches that turned out to be destroyed huts and sugar mills. On the right we saw the foothills of the Caraballo and its serrated silhouette, covered with wild vegetation.

Very close to a dark growth of cane in which there were many signs of the enemy's presence, the column halted in order to refresh the soldiers and, shortly afterward, it set out again having tightened precautions.

Chapter Ten

After entering the province of Bataan and after several days of fruitless pursuit, the column had to split into companies in order to operate in separate zones and clear them of small enemy nuclei.

I was designated head of operations and the centers of operation were Dinalupijan, a strategically placed town, and small Nijni Novgorod in the provinces of Bataan, Zambales, Pampanga and Bulacán.

I do not have a complete diary of operations undertaken in the three months spent in the town, but I have vivid memories of the fatigue we experienced as we moved through the forests on the western slope of the range that runs along the province.

The splitting up and agility of the enemy led us, as was the case in Cuba, to a pursuit without pause or rest in the springs found in the plains and in the tangled underbrush of the mountains.

We spent day after day and night after night hunting an invisible enemy. During each day's search after very difficult marches under a burning sun that beat down on the yellow fields of recently harvested rice, or after difficult climbs through intricate mountain labyrinths covered with dense, daunting undergrowth that forced us to leave the lower reaches of the mountains in order to find our way along rivers filled with rocks, or streams propelled from above down deep, stone cliffs, we invariably had to set up camp when deepening, pressing shadows moved down from the heights of the peaks, or when nature with the help of intricately tangled vegetation, or the long ago dislodgment of enormous stones blocked our passage with insurmountable obstructions.

We managed to pitch camp in unexplored places after countless strenuous attempts. To the great astonishment of the *bantays* [bearers], *indios* who carried the forces' rations, we traversed places and roads in the domain of the black *aetas*[1] who were completely unknown to them despite their proximity.

By the clear light of calm days, during moonlit nights, under the burning midday sun, in the silver glow of the moon reflected on the fronds of the foliage covered with dew, I had occasion to observe—thanks to the differing quality of the light in its many nuances—all the treasure of hidden beauty held in the labyrinthine hills of the Bataan range.

The jungle grows exuberantly over the layers of soil that cover the rocks, and its powerful sap fecundates the cracks filled with vegetal matter deposited by *baguios* [hurricanes] in the inner parts of the quartz or the granite.

It is an unstoppable irruption of life that in the viscous spilling of its splendid and fresh sap fecundates death itself. Over enormous trunks cast down by the weight of centuries, gnawed by the corrosive ferment of decomposition and death, a splendid, fresh and vigorous growth of stalks and new bushes appears.

The powerful fecundity that germinates in death, lacking terrain, sprinkles its infinite seeds everywhere and, penetrating the chaste bark, fecundates the innermost parts of the still living organism.

Over the *mangostán*, the *molave*, the *camagón* and an infinite variety of spectacular, beautiful trees, a thick web of climbing plants and parasites entwine and mix together the berries of the *euforbios*, *arecas* and strychnine trees. They hang from the leafy tops of trees in huge and showy festoons and then disappear in waves of vegetation formed by the bluebells, the narcissus, and all the disordered confusion of wandering, creeping plants.

The life of the vegetation bubbles up in the bowels of the earth and oozing out through its pores impregnates the atmosphere with that strong and penetrating odor of fermented plants exhaled by tropical forests under the ardent caress of the sun or the humid breath of the night.

Days passed and we continued to follow the itinerary marked by the traces of the enemy and lacking such traces, by trails indicated to us by inspiration.

Sometimes we camped on the banks of a torrential river, hidden behind a jumble of rocky hills; on other occasions we stopped near the pool of a river, taking advantage of the clearing in some of the forests that bordered the banks.

We tried to avoid roads and prevent being seen in order to lie in wait, in a position to carry out successful ambushes. On dark nights the cooking fires were lit very far away from the encampment. When we ran out of rations, we invariably headed for the town to rest for a night, and left again when we had replenished our stores.

The fruitless results we had obtained with the column were scarcely different when we divided the column into companies.

One night we came upon a *negrito* from a settlement of *aetas*, and from what he said, we came to suspect that the enemy must have crossed to the other slope of the sierra.

NOTE

1. Negritos was and is a common appellation for the Aeta. Considered to be among the earliest inhabitants of the Philippines, they are Australo-Melanesians who are thought to have reached the Philippines through land bridges that linked the islands with the Asian mainland. When Ricardo Burguete was in the Philippines the Aeta lived in isolated mountainous parts of Luzón.

Chapter Eleven

The western slope is more beautiful than the opposite slope due to its rough terrain.

I have already told you, reader, that I do not have a diary of operations. Therefore, I can only give you colorful impressions, faded inevitably by the undertow of time.

One night we received orders to cross the mountain range at the Malinta Pass. We spent three days of very painful marches through a terrain marked by precipices and cliffs, pressing forward at the beginning through the vast overgrowth that obstructed the slippery paths opened in the rock, camping every night along the crevices opened by tempestuous torrents. Then, leaving one morning when the ashen clouds covering the high peaks were breaking up, we managed to discern the houses of Olangopo and a bit of the bay.

Finally, our anxiety dissipated; the constant fear of losing our way on our day marches had not come true.

When we left the sharp descent and the vast jungle of the steep mountain, we came to a road through an immense mangrove swamp that led to the town. Not a living soul appeared before us in that three-day march. The *aetas negritos* abandoned their holdings when we drew near, and the silence in the imposing solitude of the sierra was disturbed at night only by the creatures that crept about in the underbrush or the flights of enormous birds that were awakened and agitated by the smoke and light of our camp fires.

When we entered Olangopo which has a superb bay and a project for a shipyard, the small garrison received us with all kinds of precautions since it did not know about our arrival and because on that same day it had received details of the crimes carried out by the insurrectionist bands and by the towns on the eastern slope that had gone over en masse to make common cause with the insurrectionists.

That same night we embarked on the steamer "Alerta" which made the crossing between Manila and Olangopo. Since it was small, the passengers were jammed onto the deck during the hours it took to reach the coastal town of Morón. It was the head of the insurrection and the amused witness to the beheading of friars and the sacking of the convent whose parishioners had played the principal role.

Disembarking was extremely difficult. The steamer approached land at some distance from the beach, which was necessitated by the depth of the water and the risks involved in the darkness of night. We had to make use of a launch that we had towed along, and that limited the operation.

Once we were opposite Morón, which the pilot determined by soundings, aided by the silhouette of hills marked by shadow, it was necessary to lower the men onto the barge and from there, after moving forward with the help of *tiquines* [bamboo sticks used instead of oars], the soldiers lowered themselves into the water, and, up to their chests in the water, they awaited the arrival of different groups in each one of the trips made by the barge.

The cold in that latitude was penetrating on contact with the water. The wait for each one of the transfers was interminable and the landing was only complete when the sound of chattering of teeth along the row of soldiers was uninterrupted.

The lights on our boat had been turned off in anticipation of our approach to land and measures were taken to muffle all noises. Not a single light indicated the presence of the town on the coast.

We guessed the proximity of the nearby beach by the sound of the waves that—moving up our chests to our armpits, making the row of soldiers unsteady—broke and died on the sand, drawing out among the dense shadows a prolonged and satisfying sigh.

After the last man had left the barge, we advanced toward dry land. When we got out of the water the cold was more intense because a light breeze made our clothes stick to our bodies. Men lay down in the sand to await the first reconnaissance patrol to venture out in the darkness.

The patrol did not take long to return, leading a corpulent *indio* who was almost completely naked, According to everyone's testimony, he came out to surrender to our forces. He said his name was Captain Domingo, the ex *gobernadorcillo* [town mayor] of Morón, and that he had escaped without any clothes, following a severe beating at the hands of the insurgents waiting for us in the town, who were aware, from what he could gather, of our arrival, judging by the rumors and movements he heard from his hiding place on the river side.

Sobbing and sounding sincere, he promised to show us the entrances to the town. Later he would speak to us about his misfortune.

Chapter Eleven

Once we understood the topography of the site, the column was divided in two: one part that would threaten the town from the shallow parts of the stream that acted as a moat, and another half that would decisively attack the wooden bridge which in the judgment of our informer was intact.

All attempts at stealth were useless. The columns had to spread out after moving forward only one hundred meters because of the sudden gun powder flashes which, amid the darkness, were set off by the diverse enemies posted on the opposite bank.

Two volleys from the column on the left simultaneously diminished the shouting and the resistance of those defending the bridge. A *bahai* next to the line of defenders illuminated their silhouettes as it burned with voracious intensity in the midst of the din caused by the firing.

The accident, whether it happened by chance or was intentional, obliged the frontline defenders to hide, and at this retreat that made the defense hesitate, our forces attacked suddenly, fired up by the cornets' calls to attack, and burst out in a rush across the bridge and the stream's shallows.

We pursued the fugitives by the light of the few flashes that illumined the street crossings. Masters of the town now, with the least cautious inhabitants finished off in their houses, people were lined up close to the convent. When our few wounded soldiers were gathered together we searched the convent standing in the middle of the dark plaza, bristling with defenses that lent it the aspect of an imposing fortress.

In order to facilitate our imminent embarkation, we set fire to the town. In the silence that followed combat it burned with sudden flames amidst the dry crackle of the bamboo and *nipa* of the towns' dwellings. The flames increased with the rapidity and voracious combustion characteristic of tow. By the light of the immense fire that cast light on a part of the plaza, a shining strip of sea was visible in whose cone of light we saw the silhouette of the "Alerta."

We proceeded to embark the various wounded men, carrying them in our arms to the launch. And by the light of the fire we picked up a dead soldier who fell into the stream from one of the bridge supports.

What a sad ceremony! It was necessary to pull him up from the bottom of the stream dripping blood and mud and, wrapped in a blanket, deposit him on the beach above the water line.

Since we had neither picks nor spades with which to bury him in the town's cemetery, it was necessary for the soldiers to dig a hole in the sand with their hands. As a grave marker we chose a heavy piece of wood embedded in the sand as the result of a shipwreck.

Shipwrecked both by a fateful storm, from that night forward both were going to sleep together in motionless and identical immobility!

Dripping blood and mud, the broken body rested at the bottom of the grave. Before throwing sand over it, I ordered the company to pray over the body of the comrade who was going to be left behind forever.

The voracious fire in the town increased the reflected light in bursts and, as the light increased, the burning material groaned, sounding like tree trunks falling and dying laments by wood that was still green.

In the midst of a horrific roar of burning houses and to cries of *Viva España!* the men ended their obsequies and, waving their hats with emotion, they then covered their bare heads to begin the embarkation.

The last handfuls of sand fell into the grave scratched out in the sand by the men's hands. We proceeded to embark in the dying glow of the fire's embers as the first light of dawn appeared on the watery horizon. As the murmuring waves advancing with the tide kissed the wood marker, inseparable from the dead man, they changed what had seemed to us before a sigh of humble satisfaction for a sound like dolorous sobbing.

Chapter Twelve

At midday we approached the Bay of Bagac, protected from observation and military attack originating from the plaza of Morón by a rocky branch of the mountain range. The Bay opens up at the foot of the jagged sierra of Mariveles, one of whose spurs hides the town from the navigators who take their ships through that corner of tranquil, green waters—water with the greenish hue of a pond caused by the reflections of the boundless greenery that struggles to take hold and finally engulfs the crags along the abrupt and narrow coastline.

We managed to disembark using the painful process followed the night before. It wasn't long before groups of people appeared on the deserted beach bearing flags and looking peaceful.

We learned through them that people had fled en masse when they found out about what happened in Morón, and that their flight was inspired by fear, unrelated to any idea of rebellion.

We went to seek lodging in the convent. The good Father had perished in the massacre in Morón and, according to what I heard from the principal figures in that municipality, the people of the town were animated by the desire for revenge because they would never pardon the wrong caused by their neighbors.

If only *they* had killed him! I thought I read this thought in the malevolent expression of those slanted eyes. —But foreigners! Never, never would those extremely faithful *indios* join the insurrection.

That town, hidden in a level space surrounded by hills, clean, pretty, with wide streets planted with trees in the style of a boulevard, served as our center of operations.

The company was lodged in the plaza: one part of it in the mayor's building and another in the convent of the unfortunate Father Dominico, who, upon leaving his rooms forever, had left in them a stamp of beatitude and order similar to that of a cell impregnated with monastic purity.

All the forces in Bataan came together to operate through the area surrounding the town and the environs of Morón.

For one month we put to the test the fidelity or the constancy of the towns' *indios* in the difficult operations of the columns' auxiliary transport. They fought with indifference when we engaged the primitive bands of insurrectionists, but all of them rivaled each other in ardor when the encounter was with their neighbors.

On one of our first marches we saw Morón again, reduced to a pile of ashes and rubble. We were helped there by the excellent guide and faithful confidant, the tall *indio* who presented himself to us stark naked on the night we left.

He was called Captain Domingo since he had exercised that charge, equivalent to mayor, in the destroyed town. The bitterness of his history guaranteed the value of his services.

On the night when the insurrection exploded and, after witnessing two assassinations, he had to flee from his house, accused of Spanish sympathies by his wife. He was a Spaniard, to be sure; however, he was always disposed to obey whoever was in charge and he would have obeyed the assassins. But the story of his Spanish sympathies was resurrected before the mob by his wife and the new mayor who, tired of insulting him with his wife's scandalous adultery and having his miserable submission serve as an impediment to his follies, decided to get rid of him, and he had to leave through a window without his clothes to seek refuge in the forest.

—Ah! He said with an expression between angry and remorseful:—I *matapan* [valiant], always fleeing without clothes to cover my shameful parts. You *babay* [wife] . . . flee with clothes, *balutari* [coffer] and *dalagas* [young maids], to cover yours up.

The unfortunate Domingo, *cabezay* [head of the village] and armed with a rifle, rivaled the explorers in valor and ardor. In those regions he was as effective as a bloodhound. Along the rivers and in the muddy areas around the deep springs in the sierra he was able to follow tracks even when they were about to be erased by the current.

One night we camped on the banks of the Aliba before one of its shallow parts in a place close to the river's mouth. The river current, lazily rolling past, fought against the sea's tide. The banks, covered with dense vegetation and relieved by small open spaces of meadow, narrowed toward the outlet to the sea until they were lost in a labyrinth of narrow gorges formed by the sierra's impenetrable rock cliffs. We fought one of the bloodiest battles in the last day's march at the lowermost part of those gaps that were sunken in dark shadow and a sinister appearance of peacefulness. The wind caused the fires that had just been lit for the mess to flicker and, at the same time, it caused the tall bamboos to sway. The fires cast a reddish light on the ground in the space illumined by a very bright moon, which, shedding light on the bare meadow facing the shallows, made a large part of the river shimmer. The foliage, which was bathed in humidity on both sides of the river, shone in the moonlight. The troops, drenched in mud and water, had to sleep through their painful injuries on the hard ground within the circuit established by the sentinels. The wounded men, distraught and querulous, waited next to a low fire for medical treatment, which I had to supply since there was no doctor. Farther off, hidden by the foliage, the livid or bloody members of the dead stuck out under a blanket. For the last time they slept that night next to their companions. Near them, the prisoners bound hand and foot and watched by sentinels, waited silent and resigned, for the light of dawn that would see the application of the just and hard law of retaliation.

Captain Domingo, who had a minor wound on his arm, lamented next to me that he hadn't been able to extract any word of consolation from the stubborn, obstinate prisoners.

No one wanted to tell him anything about his wife and daughters. And yet there was no doubt that they knew something. In the encampment we had attacked, a bloodstained skirt was found which the poor guide recognized as belonging to one of his daughters and which he did not let out of his hands, passing it before his eyes like a flag signaling his desperation.

He approached the silent group of prisoners five or six times and finally one of them talked, spitting out these words at Domingo's pained face:

"You brought *castila* [Spaniard], and he kill your daughter. But I no know. Blood on skirt tell you everything: either she is wounded or she on path followed by her mother." Domingo howled in pain, throwing himself on the *tao* (*indio*). His cries awakened the soldiers nearby who helped the sentinels separate him from the string of prisoners, all of whom he wanted to kill.

In the serene, clear night the rising tidal waters murmured in the brush on the riverbanks.

The breeze, laden with salts and emanations from the mud, with its querulous swaying stirred the erect and plumed bamboos, and occasionally drew out from the depth of the forests the scent of *ilang-ilang* whose sweetness, in the course of the night, masked the stench of decomposition and death that the corrosive humidity produced in the bloody, rigid corpses under the blankets.

Tending to the wounded lasted until very late for lack of resources. It must have been dawn when the column headed for the beach, carrying among its number the sad and dolorous convoy of dead and wounded, placed in blankets or hammocks.

In the town, still deserted and burned out, the wooden structures creaked under their own weight and, as we passed by, some fell down noisily, raising clouds of ash.

The beach spread out before our eyes and sparkled under the sun's rays with the infinite reflection of the shells and silica in its sands. The enormous piece of wood, covered with algae on the part closest to the water, was swollen, serving as a bulwark for the sand dug up for the first grave, and in its absolute immobility seemed fixed there to guard and defend the unfortunate shipwrecked men from squalls from the sea and from life. Ah! Combatted constantly by the waves, who knows what sad adventures it alone witnessed through the years and even the centuries!

We again performed the dismal ceremony with which in recent days we had bidden farewell to our companions on the coast of Bagac at Olangopo. Over the sand dug up for the graves of our newly dead a sharp volley of shots exploded the craniums of the prisoners, causing them to fly like bits of pasteboard over the sand.

We left the beach to continue operations by moving into the forest. The vultures that had followed us on the march flew in circles above the dead prisoners whose blood stained the uniform color of the coast, which was bathed in sun and brightened by multiple reflections drawn from the shells and stones that, jostled by the incoming tide, struck together noisily, singing below the foaming waves a restless and calming hymn.

Chapter Thirteen

We returned to Dinalupijan, the municipal seat of our zone. The detachment from the small blockhouses that we had left to defend the approaches to the town came out to receive us along with the soldiers, the public, and a commission of the principal figures in the town who also came out to the road. News of the pacification on the opposite side of the mountain was circulated before we arrived. That success boosted our authority so that we were received amidst cheers, flags, music and other excesses.

The fiestas and attentions lasted long enough to provide the time necessary for the troops to recuperate before setting out to fight enemy nuclei dispersed on the other side of the mountain.

The game of *panguingui* [a card game] was permitted, *cucañas* [greased poles competition] were raised in the plaza, and, to the sound of musicians who roved tirelessly through the streets, the plebe got its fill of dancing[1] the *gubli*, the *cutang-cutang*, the *osé*, the *estejarro*, and even the *culitangán* and the *moro-moro*, imported from Jolo.

The principal figures came to serve the table in our lodging and, in the plaza in order to celebrate their own people, they provided a good number of *carejais* [pots] and other vessels replete with *morisqueta* [rice], with water buffalo milk, and *dinuguan* [blood pudding]. Slop—after it got cold—that was served indiscriminately at the end of the day to people and dogs.

We organized a dance in the convent, which served us as a barracks since the indigenous priest was not there. It was attended by the daughters of the *cabezay* [deputy mayors]: Totay (Carlota), Wena (Eugenia), Guicay (Francisca), Charin (Rosario), Pelan (Rafaela), Chate (Manuela), Asón (Consolación). These were the most select of the *dalagas* [single women], with their hair loose down their backs, adorned with beads and sequins and decked out in the showiest colors in dresses and *chapines* [slippers].

The *dalagas and matandas* [young women and old women] left late at night, very pleased with the celebration.

Once the fiesta and the music ended, I looked out from one of the dark windows of the convent. I saw that the departing women formed a line and, turning their backs to the building, lifted the front of their dresses with one hand and with the other carefully lifted the train of the dress . . . A sudden shower made me step back from the observatory fearing the rain. I looked at the firmament, which starry and serene, shone with luminous winks at seeing the upright female partisans satisfy a necessity with the violence of a sudden squall in the most unusual and capricious manner that the amused reader could imagine.

NOTE

1. I have not found any source that describes the dances listed here.

Chapter Fourteen

When we had rested for a few days and were ready to begin new operations, telegrams from Manila summoned us back to the capital in order to take part in the invasion of the province of Cavite, after concluding that our province was pacified.

The town bade us farewell and, after three months away we started back. We undertook the march along the dusty road that we had followed earlier, protected from the sun by the clouds in a gray and overcast morning.

At the end of our day's march, close to the great Pampanga River, we saw ahead of us ruined cane fields and burned out huts off in the distance. The sky and firmament were of a uniform color, desolate and sad. I turned my gaze to the column that was marching at a rapid pace, and at the sight of the foggy, jagged mountains of Bataan obscuring the horizon, I stopped, invaded by sadness, to count the number of those men who, in hospitals or imprisoned forever in the sands of the beach, were missing in the return march along that dusty road.

The first houses in Florida Blanca appeared and, after passing a line of huts, the attractive house belonging to Señor N, appeared . . . How sad! How different from before! Waiting for us in the portico, three of his daughters, dressed in severe mourning, took us to the room where their father was convalescing from his latest heart attack. In only three months, implacable death had carried off the youngest daughter and in passing, left behind, along with grief, paralysis in her poor father's legs.

Burned out hopes showed in the old man's face with the same ashen color that covered the remains of the once flourishing cane fields.

It was difficult for him to speak about his misfortunes, and the congratulations he expressed on our campaign ended in a fit of breathlessness that plunged him into a profound dejection. He recovered, pausing often to voice sad prophecies:

—We were leaving never to meet again ... The war was still raging under the surface and the small bands of insurrectionists that we thought were extinguished would prove to be sparks charged with spreading the fire freely. The submission of the *indio* would be the best combustible ... The same thing would happen in Cavite and then in all parts of the archipelago ... Spain would be strong enough to quench the flames of the bonfire, but it would leave the hatred of three centuries of abandonment and injustice to ignite again in the embers ... He would not be lucky enough to see his family perish together in the midst of a general catastrophe ... He would die and the orphans, consumed by the illnesses and deceits of that perfidious country would perhaps survive only to have their virtue go up in flames in the disaster ...

We left the house with heavy hearts, pushed on by the pressing order that summoned us to Manila.

The clouds wept a light rain which, splashing on the dusty road, soon began to cover it entirely

I looked back at the chalet and at the top of the steps I saw the silhouettes of the bereaved orphans who were crying silently, waving at us through the veil of implacable weeping falling more heavily from the firmament and beginning to drown the fields on the left and right of the mud-covered surface of the roadway.

The troops covered themselves with their blankets and, after crossing a banana plantation whose broad leaves shivered, limp, and contracted in the rain, we continued along the edges of the town, along the road that threatened to turn into a canal under the persistent weeping of the ashen sky.

During those sad, cloudy moments, casting aside bodily discomforts, my afflicted spirit insistently recalled the verses of a dear friend:

> "Certain rainy days produce
> sadness in my soul; doubtless there are clouds that hold
> the moisture of tears."

Chapter Fifteen

Events unfolding in the war and preparations for the campaign underway in Cavite had affected the spirits of the people and led to a state of febrile impatience and unusual activity that affected normal life in Manila.

For several days the agglomeration of peninsular battalions in the capital exceeded the idle troops on the streets and avenues.

The dominant note on the streets comprised the Peninsular and the indigenous soldier. The former walked in groups of comrades who out of habit marched along in guerrilla mode, expressing idle curiosity. The indigenous soldier always walked alone, he was short, agile and alert, dressed in a striped uniform, European style, but different because his pants were rolled up so that from the knee down his legs and bare feet were visible.

The city took on the aspect of a military encampment given the exercises of the troops on foot, the mounted forces or the recently formed bands that participated noisily in the constant parades through the walled city or the outskirts. The presence of battalions of volunteers and the innumerable guerrillas recruited through casinos and guilds also stirred peoples' spirits and, driven by the immediacy of what was happening, led to conversations on the exclusive topic of the war.

My good friend Argüelles brought me up to date on recent events: Bulacán, La Laguna, the hills of San Mateo and all the big nuclei of the insurrection were almost pacified, except for the province of Cavite which remained intact and fortified in the power of the insurrectionists, who had accumulated all kinds of resources and, in the judgment of our spies, had increased the ranks of defenders in the rebel bands dispersed in other provinces. The insurrection was not lacking spirit, for days earlier they had dared, along with their *generalísimo* Aguinaldo to approach the gates of Manila, and when they were repulsed still tried to cross the Pasig, in order to invade northern Luzón.

Cacarong de Siler, the fight at Las Lomas de San Mateo, and many other victories for our arms had not served to chasten them, but they did serve to increase reasons for mourning in the *mestizo* and indigenous population of the city.

I took note of my friend's observation. I saw that, in fact, innumerable women wore black headdresses, and since my departure the number of young Malay women[1] wearing muslin bands on their arms, the customary way of indicating mourning, had increased markedly.

The war had imposed its destructive disruption on the Oriente Hotel and, as a consequence, the elegance and serene peace of the first days had disappeared. There was a strong odor of iodoform and phenol along the wide hallways with their sumptuous wooden floors and through some half-open doors. I learned that many wounded officers for whom the stay in hospital was a cruel torture had been able after repeated requests to secure rooms in the hotel.

The pretty ex-governor, on her way back to Spain, did not witness these horrors. Through that same half-visible room that her absence left vacant, I saw the open door and, in the semi-darkness, a crack of light that the half-closed window cast on the mirror allowed me to see the familiar bed. Scattered on the floor at the foot of the bed, I saw thick bundles of cotton wool of some wounded patient, whose moans I thought I could hear in the dark recesses of the room.

The events of the war and preparations for the campaign had disturbed the ambient peace and the luminous serenity of the sky that, amidst flare-ups of fire or a multitude of small embers, enveloped Manila in the tranquil succession of days and nights.

Crowds and the main sites of agitation were located on the central streets of the outskirts or along the Bridge of Spain. The old city, inside the belt of its walls covered with leprous-like moss, lifted the towers of its convents into space. With the incessant monotonous ringing of its bells, it lulled the canonical somnolence of those ancient streets of old Manila, invaded day and night by devotion and shade.

Fear was depopulating the chalets situated in the outskirts and the picturesque estates on the banks of the river. Abandoned by their owners, the picturesque dwellings all along the roadways, pretty and contrite in their deserted and desolate appearance, seemed to weep at their abandonment amidst the fainting banana plants and palms, pressed by the embrace of climbing, anarchic vegetation whose dense jungle odor robbed the atmosphere of the sweet aroma of *ilang-ilang* and jasmine.

One night, on the Paseo de la Luneta, they took me to the corner where the last executions by firing squads had taken place. The Paseo was very crowded and a light layer of dust hovered over the passersby. It shone in the light and was not dispersed by the breeze from the sea whose sounding waves died at the foot of the coach path.

Standing on the dry ground that had received the bloody bodies of the convicted men, they told me details of the drama that the most spirited men underwent with stoical serenity, while other men had to be carried like bundles to the spot; and there was one man—his name doesn't matter—who had to be transported to the place of execution in a basket.

On the wings of the wind a shower of notes reached us of a pleasing piece that the musicians were performing in the kiosk next to the dusty promenade. Beyond the promenade, the coastline became visible and was then lost to sight far away in enemy territory. We were aware of the enemy's presence because of the sight of innumerable bonfires that shone in the darkness beyond and on the surface of the sea with angry and threatening reflections.

NOTE

1. In the 1880s and 1890s, inhabitants of the Philippines were generally divided by foreigners into two groups, the Malay "race" and the *negritos*. Subdivisions of the Malays included *indios*, Chinese *mestizos*, and the much smaller group of Spanish *mestizos*. See D. J. Walker, *Representations of the Cuban and Philippine Insurrections on the Spanish Stage, 1887–1898* (Tempe, AR: Bilingual Press, 2001), 96–107, for a discussion of the views of Ricardo Burguete's contemporaries on the racial divisions in the Archipelago.

Chapter Sixteen

The capital began to be cleared of troops. All along the left bank of the Pasig River the battalions and brigades that would form the troops invading Cavite were taking positions. According to the plan of the General in chief, one brigade would threaten the line of the Zapote River, while the division of the left flank (two brigades) would go to the foothills of the Sungay and, following the downward slope of the terrain, would cover the aforementioned river, attacking from the rear and, along the flank, overcoming obstacles of the terrain and the fortifications raised by the enemy.

The campaign that was prepared during the preceding months was expected to produce marvelous results.

Judging by the results of the preparatory works planned in cabinet, the terrible equation of the war would be solved in our favor. Against all the auxiliary forces of the insurrection, there would be an accumulation of troops and resources organized with patient and farseeing care:

Would the full cooperation of individual and collective human effort in implementing the plan for our troops lead to favorable results?

Here is the unknown factor in warfare that also introduces uncertainty into the most sublime conceptions of art. The wearing down of a tool or its incorrect use, however brief it might be, is enough to ruin the best -conceived work of the artist.

All along the river, a few miles from Manila, the Peninsular and indigenous battalions camped or bivouacked, occupying the barricades and unpopulated spaces of an extensive stretch of land that reached as far as Pateros. Mixed in with them in barracks and animal pens, the cavalry and the units that were recently organized waited together with the engineers, ambulance, and military administration under whose control all the materiel indispensable for the advance was concentrated.

Beside the river whose banks were festooned with bushes and scrub amidst erect tufts of bamboo whose cane shoots were moving downward into the slow-moving current of the broad channel, the ambulant vendors had set up innumerable stands that lent the encampment the festive appearance characteristic of a popular pilgrimage.

The soldiers chatted or formed small groups in which troops, defensive forces, and auxiliary arms mixed together.

Through the windows of the houses, groups of troops or improvised gatherings of officers appeared next to tables in their lodgings.

The march along the straight road that ran parallel to the river was difficult because of the groups that gathered around the vendors' stands; because of the comings and goings of soldiers; and because of the innumerable wagons carrying volunteers or curiosity seekers that lined up behind the wagons, the mules and the whole jumble of means of transport that, authorized for war service, would constitute the supply convoy. Carts and people stood away from the road at times to let the mounted squads pass by, enveloped in a column of dust. On the river the small steamers that made the crossing to Laguna province came and went regularly; the ones going upriver were taking all the materiel that the Sangay division would need. Amidst harsh and prolonged whistles of sirens, welcomed with applause and enthusiastic cries by the soldiers on the river banks, fast-moving steamers unobstructed by masts and spars on deck, cut through the gentle current, carrying platoons of soldiers who waved their hats in greeting. They also carried war materiel such as wagons for transporting and mounting cannon, gun carriages, cases, and mortars arranged in compact piles. Stretching their necks above the railings, the ears of mules and horses stood erect out of fear and, at the same time, fear made the poor beasts' eyes open very wide with alarm when they saw the many fast-moving remnants of frayed canes in the water loosened from the river banks.

Throughout the day the crossing of steamers did not stop. They disappeared in a turn of the river amidst plumes of smoke. In the turmoil of getting underway the Spanish flags on the poop decks were unfurled to the wind with sonorous resoluteness.

Even more vendor stands appeared on the road where dust kicked up by the incessant coming and going floated in the atmosphere. The sun's rays, pouring out fire, fell like lead on the heads of the soldiers, lighting up the multitude of straw hats. The smoke from the fires lit in each of the encampments along the road was carried along by the wind, adding to the stifling, burning atmosphere.

All the conversations between soldiers and officers turned on the same theme: the past operations; the risks run; the fatigue and penalties of the zone they had just left.

Chapter Sixteen

For everyone, the actions of their battalions and even the personal actions of each narrator exceeded that of their listeners. Inflamed by disputes and bets in that atmosphere rarefied by dust and smoke, in the midst of the infernal ruckus of shouts, orders and voices, the groups grew animated and a few drops of alcohol were enough to inflame those heads imprisoned in the *paveros de yarey* [hats of woven palm leaf] that glittered in the sun.

As I walked around, I heard men making pacts and betting on atrocities. No man doubted the success of the campaign and, in order to affirm his own importance, it was enough in the heat of enthusiasm and discussion to tout his own efforts.

The indigenous soldiers chatted barefooted and silent, or in groups they washed their clothes and bodies at the riverside.

The coming and going of coaches and mounted patrols continued without let- up, pushing groups on foot to the side of the road. The whistle of the sirens cutting through the air beside the river, matched the bugles and cornets that called each one of the corps and units to its division or service.

In the evening as fiery-red clouds were reflected in the waters of the Pasig River, the auxiliary Chinese brigade[1] passed in front of my lodgings carrying on their shoulders pieces of quartered cattle, which were gushing blood. The brigade distributed the meat to the soldiers, and for a long time there hung in the air of the reddish twilight a nauseating odor of skinned flesh and slaughter. In a corral that spread out before me, the cattle belonging to the infantry rubbed against each other, pawing the ground impatiently, and farther off four shining bronze cannons with threatening pendants, were lined up correctly, watched over by two sentinels.

The afternoon was declining and along the road recently bloodied by the convoy of quartered meat, groups gathered again and resumed the ardent tone of their conversations.

Within sight of the ground stained with blood that was beginning to disappear under the foot traffic, in the midst of the burning heat filled with cries, sharp notes of cornets and out of tune sounds of bugles, breathing the dusty air impregnated with the stench of slaughter, I felt the heat of an ardor identical to that of the groups of soldiers rise up from the depths of my being, and the residue of the primitive beast, the ebullience of the *norso* [Norse man] caught fire in my blood and coursed through my arteries, urging me to destroy, to shout, to commit acts of savagery.

Would the campaign succeed? Yes. There was no question about it. The ardor behind its execution would assure the triumph of the well-thought-out plan.

The first shadows of night dissipated my doubts and the vivid clarity of the distant glowing bonfires lit for the soldiers' messes ignited my faith.

Ah! How different is the roar of a rousing, well-prepared war from the slow, silent and sterile sacrifice that took place in Cuba! Death threatens the two fields of battle equally, but how different to die just around a bend, face down in the dip of a ditch, as opposed to falling within sight of everyone while going beyond the common efforts of the other soldiers; to die in the din of combat, while experiencing the inebriation of vanity consecrated to enflaming the valor of the warrior!

I evoked other times, other ages. The vast encampment with the multiple lights of the vehicles and the small lamps of the vendors' stands, brought to mind the image of a warrior tribe camping on the road, preparing for a bloody invasion that would end in the extermination of the enemy. Gigantic shadows cast by innumerable small lanterns spread out in the *lusco y fusco* [twilight] under the starry sky. Along the plumes of bamboo that adorned the road, in the midst of the infernal shouting, I thought I discerned a portion of Norman forest controlled by a legion of warriors from the North—the *norso,* the barbarian, whom our civilization detests. He lived there and then and, unfortunately, he will live on among all of us who inhabit our miserable human shell.

Pride makes us detest war only to suffer more cruelly the imposition of its torments. The *norso* had a god, Thor, and made a religion of war. That religion, rude, grave, but sincere, seems grim to us. Yet, the consecration of valor—writes Carlyle[2]—was sufficient for those ancient and valiant *norsos*.

But this same war that civilization curses only to engage in it nonetheless, does not have among its religions the consolation of the semi-barbaric paganism that justified all causes placed at the service of valor and effort. Paganism made use of the Valkyries to separate those men who sacrificed themselves heroically from among the mountains of dead and lead them on to a better life.

The siren blast of a steamer that was crossing the river resounded like an enormous war conch, prompting a band of vultures on the roof of my lodging to flap their wings. In anticipation of our operations they were, in turn, taking up positions next to us.

Cornets and bugles called out the retreat and the road began to clear.

I returned to reality, forgetting the legend of the Valkyries. Humanitarian, pious civilization discarded the pagan fantasy, but it could not discard war. It taught that it was fitting only for vultures and crows—which were at the time puffing up their feathers on the roof of my lodging—to visit men killed in combat in order to select them from the heaps of the dead and peck arbitrarily at the glassy eyes of their purplish, bloodied corpses.

Chapter Sixteen

NOTES

1. Ricardo Burguete does not provide any information on the Chinese brigade mentioned here, and in chapters 18 and 19, except to note that they were part of auxiliary transport. In his *Campaña de Filipinas; la división Lachambre* (Madrid: Librería de Hernando y Compañía, 1898), Federico de Monteverde y Sedano referred to the transport components in General Lachambre's campaign to pacify Cavite in 1897. These components, he wrote, were drawn from the countryside itself given the immediate need for them. In addition to carts and small native horses, transport relied upon Chinese manpower. Monteverde y Sedano added:

> And finally, the campaign used the Chinese in considerable numbers, They walked in pairs and carried the rations secured on long, cylindrical poles, called *pingas*, which were held on their shoulders. Those poles and rations typically fell to the ground at the sound of the first shot. Yet, it is not our intention to offend the *Sons of Heaven*. With honorable exceptions, the whistle of a bullet passing above their pig-tailed heads, frightened them so, that they threw down their load and, bunched together and running fast, they tried to position themselves far from the column where the shots originated. Their guards were hard put to gather them together, oblige them to pick up the rations, and comply with the arrangement they had voluntarily entered into and for which they were very well paid.
>
> [Y por último, utilizáronse los chinos en cantidad suficiente, quienes por parejas y colgando de largos palos cilíndricos, a que llaman *pingas*, colocados sobre sus hombros, conducían las raciones, que de seguro caían por los suelos al sonar el primer disparo, pues sin que en nuestro ánimo entre la intención de ofender a los *Hijos del Cielo* y salvo honrosas excepciones, el silbido de alguna bala más o menos alta sobre sus trenzadas cabezas les producía tal miedo, que arrojaban las cargas y apelotonados y a la carrera procuraban replegarse al sitio opuesto de la columna en que sonaban los tiros, siendo preciso a sus escoltas grandes esfuerzos para contenerlos, obligarlos a recoger las raciones y a que cumpliesen el compromiso voluntariamente contraído y muy bien pagado.] (299–301)

See the illustration in this book captioned "A Chinese man bearing rations in the convoys." Monreverde y Sedano listed under "Means of Transport in The Army of the Island of Luzón," "Media Brigada [Half Brigade]; 600 Chinese and as many more as might be recruited in the territory under the command of the General of the Division" (*Campaña de Filipinas*, 105).

2. Thomas Carlyle (1795–1881) was a Scottish writer whose influence in his lifetime and beyond was far reaching. Burguete's references to Norsemen, Thor, war, the role of the Valkyries, and the supreme importance of valor echo Carlyle's treatment of these topics in the first lecture "The Hero as Divinity. Odin. Paganism: Scandinavian Mythology" of his *Heroes, Hero-Worship, and the Heroic in History: Six Lectures* (London: James Fraser, 1841).

Chapter Seventeen

It was necessary to provide plans and a location for the forces. When the brigade of Zapote was left isolated, we began to form part of it and planned to lodge in Culi-Culi.

Very near the town, we improvised a hut with palm fronds and banana leaves that we replaced every day thanks to the near-by banana plantation.

Our situation as the vanguard of the general line of the brigade demanded painful duty on the days that preceded the operations.

At night, especially, it was necessary to establish ambushes and listening outposts along the roads and, as a result of these precautions, we succeeded in catching the numerous enemy confidents and spies who ventured to cross the lines with messages.

The maneuver was extremely onerous and required interminable nights of waiting when, in order to stifle all sounds, at the slightest movement in the forest we silenced our breathing by lying close to the ground or by stifling the sounds of breathing with fistfuls of foliage. Snakes slithered through the grass and their passage made us tremble with emotion, making our hearts pound in our chests. Several of the spies whom we captured paid with their lives for the risky job they undertook on the dry grass of beds improvised for a night of spying in the recesses of the forest. It wasn't possible to make them confess the object of their mission and, after a quick trial with a foregone conclusion, their lives and their secrets would be swallowed up at a forest crossroads at the break of day.

One morning after the previous evening's preparations, we had to undertake a march, flanking the rest of the brigade that had left Pateros. We were going to undertake the march through the desert limited by the Laguna de Bay in front of us and by the Zapote River. We took the precaution of having the troops cut cane tubes in the jungle for carrying water, which we would not find in the day's march.

The desert is formed by a succession of plateaus of fissured, sandy terrain that made marching difficult and impeded our progress. Some tufts of sparse, dry vegetation stain the vast surface of that yellowish sea, cut through by hills and depressions that resemble gigantic waves of sand. The sandy dust dislodged by our feet during the march, was heated by the sun before it stuck to the sweat on our bodies or entered with every breath into our noses and mouths. We used up the water in the cane tubes during the first hours of the march, and soon the dry air our panting lungs were breathing in made all of us participating in the flanking operation extremely thirsty.

The main column, which was far off, folded and unfolded sinuously on the hill like a big worm with shining scales. Two or three times, on the high part of a steep slope we were able to see the artillery and the equipment that, like the enormous belly of a reptile, gleamed in the sun with the glossy brightness of multiple little mirrors.

The cavalry stood out in long lines that moved along sniffing about like insect antennae. It was necessary at midday to give the troops a rest. We selected the top of a hill from which we managed to see in the distance the enormous extension of the lake, limited by a faint line of hills and ruffled with waves—which increased our tormenting thirst.

—Water! Water! The cry came from the column. The image of that blue surface that lightly bathed in humidity the first mouthfuls of a breeze that refreshed us on the little hill, served to kindle and irritate desire.

It was vain to hope that we could approach the edges of the lake. The march began again turning to the right in order not to abandon the dividing line where we thought that we would meet the first resistance on the part of the enemy.

The torture increased at the sight of the distant water. The slightly moistened breeze sweetened the palate for a moment, leaving behind an impression of fire in the throat.

The sun burned our heads while our heated and wide-ranging imaginations turned all eyes to the lake and tortured us with fanciful delights that did not satiate desire.

During the march I felt my legs become unsteady every time I stumbled on the cracked terrain. I tried not to look at the water, but it was useless! My imagination savored delights that ended by burning my palate and my tongue with such dry irritation that I had to breathe in with open mouth the faint emanations of fresh air that the sun dried up immediately. I ended up giving my senses and my mind free rein, and with the kind of fantasies dreamed up by a somnambulist, I walked on for a distance. My imagination drank in the lake; first I wet my lips, then I took small sips and finally, not satisfied with single draughts of sweet, crystalline water, I drank entire waves, and finished by completely drinking up the source of the water and drinking mud instead. I heard buzzing in my ears and felt sharp pains in my tonsils that moved up inside my ears.

Sharp, distant shots drew our eyes to the mounted forces, which stood out against the blue depths of the horizon amidst little clouds of smoke. The column as it approached us was more visible and we interpreted the brilliant scales of the reptile as the reflection of the arms and mess tins of the troops.

Soon we would enter the demarcation of Almansa, a fortified enemy site and the end of this stage of our march if we were able to attack it. On one of the heights of the dividing line we were following, I glanced at the landscape. In front of us the Sungay rose above the line of mountains that rimmed the Laguna. Like a trench, the line of vegetation of the Zapote extended to the right and, forming a line along our right flank the white walls of the towns of Paranaque, the Piñas and Cavite were concealed in the distance by a curving line of greenery bordering the sea.

At sunset we reached the road and followed the tracks of the principal column whose advance guard had just reached the huts of Almansa without encountering any resistance. A reddish dust, whose color was intensified by the reflection of the setting sun, covered the road, and we stepped onto it as if it were a plush rug, our feet being accustomed to the rough terrain of the desert.

To our left and far away, to add to the cruelty of our thirst, a rifle shot ruffled the waters of the lake. During the last part of the march I walked like an automaton, tormented by a severe headache, opening and closing my eyes to visions of light.

Very close to the abandoned trenches of Almansa, a green, viscous pool guarded by a cordon of sentinels prevented us from going near it. We crossed by it and on the edges of the muddy water, hot with fever, I plunged my feet and arms into the pond.

If I hadn't lived through the hours of that night I would never have experienced the perception of eternal time. We camped in one of the forts closest to the viscous pool, which was used only to bathe water buffalo. At the first sign of evening shadows I lay down on the straw floor of a hut, seized by intense, febrile cold. There was no hope of drinking even a drop of water. The troops could not prepare the mess and had to eat the meat of water buffalo roasted in the bonfires without any water.

I recall the blurry, delirious impression of that night. The corps medic came to see me and after he took my pulse he ordered that I be given iodine to reduce the inflammation in my throat.

The first hours were horribly cruel. My feverish thirst and the horrible dryness of my throat whose swollen tissue prevented me from swallowing was about to drive me mad.

Why was that happening? Why were we encamped without water? I didn't find out why then, and I don't know why now, but that night I did become aware of the stages that reason passes through to arrive at a state of delirium. Shaken by the intense cold of my fever, I thought I was carried to the middle of the muddy pool and every time I bent down to drink the greenish liquid I sank into a well without bottom, whose depth increased with every effort I made and ended by taking my breath away. Shortly afterwards, the vision of the Laguna tormented me. I had been able to reach it on the sly, dragging myself along, outwitting the cordon of sentinels, but it was useless! A vain attempt! I could not drink the water because the edges of the lake were scorched earth that burned the palms of my hands. I returned to the road. In my delirium, my feverish imagination showed me a hidden well with water shining at the bottom. I lowered myself into it breaking the bones of my hands and feet with my efforts until disappointment erased my false illusion. My hand only reached handfuls of blackish mud; at the bottom the reflection of a shining star fooled me into thinking it was the reflection of light on water.

I recalled biblical thirst, the thirst of the deserts. The horrible thirst experienced in caravans that, after running out of the blood of the camels, fought over human blood. In the end, I too drank blood, and my palate registered its warm, nauseating taste. Whose blood was it?

My imagination went to sleep and desire, irritated to the point of paroxysm, drained my sensitiveness. Now water surrounded me everywhere and refreshed my palate, but I could not drink it because of my swollen throat. For a moment I did not feel thirst, the repugnance and fullness of the very mouthful I had drunk that morning rose to my mouth, and so, because of the repugnance I felt—a reflection of my exhausted sensitiveness—I managed to rest a few hours until the beginning of the new day.

On the horse that a companion lent me on our return, I slept through the torpor brought on by my fever . . . I recall that a few steps from the accursed encampment there were some wells that slaked the mad thirst of the soldiers, as well as my own and provided us with enough to fill our cane tubes.

The march back to Parañaque was extremely painful for me. The terrain, the fields, the hills we climbed the day before, went round and round in my head which threatened to burst, gripped by fever and heated by the sweat pouring out of it under the sun's rays.

In the last hour of the day's march, the enemy, having set fire to the extremely dry brush in the fields, was at the point of wiping out the rearguard which counted by the dozens cases of sudden asphyxia.

Chapter Eighteen

One morning the general staff arrived in Parañaque.

The impression of the last march was still red hot in my body and spirit.

Thirst, the horrible thirst we had experienced, in the judgment of the experts had saved lives in the conquest and occupation of Almansa. Ah, those calculations made in cabinet failed in the end because they did not take into account the limits of human resistance. Suffocation on our return cost the lives of more men than those who would have died defending the town. On the Chinese brigade alone that was in charge of transport, death feasted greedily:

—Opium! Opium! *Señolía,*—and suddenly taking on the yellowish color of amber, they lay down, their bodies rigid on the ground, and we had to put them on the backs of mules to get them away from the fires the enemy had just ignited.

A death without glory, without sacrifice, with no other effort expended than that of life escaping abundantly through their pores since it couldn't leave through their suffocated breathing. The Valkyries would certainly not come to take away the most glorious of those prosaic dead men. Not even the vultures or the crows that followed us on the march dared to venture into the dense layer of smoke that enveloped us.

Preparations continued in headquarters for the assault on Pamplona. Once we were masters of that place, we would be masters of the parallel line that would threaten Zapote.

The night before our departure the soldiers were given assignments and those of us who were to form part of the vanguard hastened to receive our direct instructions from the general staff.

When we left the convent where the general in chief was lodged, we crossed a patio where toward the rear we saw the enormous parts of the *tren de sitio*[1] that had been brought from Manila with unheard-of difficulty.

The companions who were waiting for us at the door came out and, as they peppered us with questions, all of us decided to spend the night on a care-free bender.

We made the rounds of all the lodgings and it was imperative to drink in each one. Mumbling a toast, and with Odin and barbarous paganism on my mind, in the company of other officers, I eventually stretched out briefly on a backpack near the soldiers from our company who had been snoring tranquilly from early on in the night.

Dawn broke, in my opinion, in the blink of an eye and reveille roused me with a general creaking of bones. The troops came out silently and sleepily from their lodgings and forming along the street, coffee was distributed to them in the dim light of the fire where it had been boiled. The first breezes of the morning finally awakened me with a sharp sensation of cold. I took a cup of coffee from what was provided to the troops and, while I awaited orders I reflected on the ones that were communicated to me the night before:

"The enemy had gathered the principal nucleus of its defenses in Pamplona and it was necessary to take control of them at all cost. The work of the vanguard must be to explore and wait, in case the effort of the defense is insuperable, until the brigade should arrive in full force."

The entire column consisted of five battalions, three batteries and soldiers on horseback. I reviewed in my imagination the mental map of the terrain I had been given. And after innumerable calculations the question of the cruel uncertainty that would be resolved in a few hours came to mind:

—Would the effort be sufficient?

When day broke we left the town by way of some planted fields and in less than a kilometer we traversed the bridges made of Indian cane that facilitated our passage over a marshy inlet. The column marched on in silence and in the distance arms shone like little mirrors in the first rays of morning light. The terrain was all planted field, cracked and muddy. Far off, the groves of bamboo cut capriciously into the horizon.

Impatience and fear made the whole vanguard stay quiet and step up the pace as it moved forward. The first platoons spread out to sniff around in the forests and ravines.

The day dawned smiling and a joyful sun bathed the broad extension of the planted fields: we crossed a small *pinac* [swamp] over a cane bridge and came upon a ravine furrowed with some trickles of water and replete with vegetation that appeared to be a component of the defensive zone around the town. When we left it, I was struck by my recollection of the map of Pamplona and with deep emotion I communicated my impressions to the commandant of the vanguard . . .

Chapter Eighteen

Before us, we could barely make out a line of houses and in front of that line a strip of earth that was a different color indicating that the soil had been dug up. We kept on advancing and as the column was moving on beyond the crest of the ravine, the huts and lines of fortifications became more visible. The first two companies spread out and, since the first remained in reserve, I lined up with them, the left flank closing the distance between the spread-out forces.

Orders were given in low voices. Curse words and blasphemies alone were audible, uttered by hoarse voices. A solemn silence and a sinister, threatening calm pressed down upon the countryside.

To the left, on the planted field bathed in light, a dense thicket of bamboo stirred by the breeze moved its upright plumes tragically, forebodingly at our passage, along with a sonorous shudder that contrasted with the calm of the surrounding space.

The line of fortifications became more distinct and shortly, the crest of the parapets appeared outlined in the blue space by a sudden succession of small clouds of smoke that sent a spray over our heads while at the same time we heard a sporadic clatter of distant firing. It was necessary to accelerate our march and the troops, lowering their heads in the shower, quickened their pace. Very soon the fire covered the enemy trenches with a dense, uniform gas. It was not possible to advance without returning fire and the spread-out forces kneeling on the ground broke out in a violent volley of firepower over the entrenchment.

As a result of a push that opened spaces in the lines, causing men to roll around on the ground, we gained one hundred meters and with our push the furious fire from the defensive forces revived. It was necessary to spread out on the left and attack a redoubt in front of us, which, standing out from the general line of trenches enclosed a cloud of heads seen through the openings in the smoke. We couldn't have been more than six hundred meters away and, at that distance, it was necessary to advance without hesitation. We advanced in small leaps in the midst of growing, anxious agitation. The din of the firing blocked our own voices. In each one of the advances, openings appeared in the line and men rolled on the ground like ramrods, leaving openings that were closed very quickly by the defensive instincts of the soldiers.

—Onward! Onward!

It was necessary to close the distance between us and our enemies. Men struck blows, howled with panting cries, and made an extraordinary effort as if they were trying to conquer an insuperable height. We were conquering the most difficult height for mankind: the heights of death!

—Onward! Onward!

Anger and fear brought out strange grimaces on the intensely pale faces of the men. The wounded men howled furiously and anyone who stood up and retreated was shot indiscriminately.

—Onward! Onward!

It was mandatory to advance, to swallow death, to go in search of it and panting, suck it in.

The redoubt was vomiting fire. The hats or the bare heads of the defenders showed amid the rents in the smoke.

—Onward! Onward!

The troops were shooting, maddened by mortal anxiety; with trembling eagerness they pulled out cartridges from their belts and advanced without stopping, scattering munitions, falling down, panting here and there with a rifle in their nervous hands and, as they fell, biting clods of earth and dust.

—Onward! Onward!

The men's exhausted physical strength or their morale, lost amidst the splashes of blood of their companions and wounded men, was deplorable.

—Onward! Onward!

Bludgeoning, blows, imprecations that shook their bodies and healed the feebleness of their spirits or compensated for the weakness of fear, resounded mercilessly:

—Onward! Onward! With our advances their defense increased and, in view of that development, anxiety and exhaustion threatened to wear down our courage:

—Onward! Onward!

The most high-spirited men were shouting and echoing the command . . . Suddenly, at the same time, an unexpected, enormous explosion that vomited fire in our direction provoked a storm of steel that ripped open the ground at our feet. Another blast followed . . . and another. The culverins and guns of the redoubt swept clear the passage way and in a moment the guerrilla retreated, swept along like a rag carried by the wind or like a sail that a hurricane shakes and twists:

—Onward! Onward!

A supreme effort was necessary: we stepped over the fallen men and the command forced men to stand up by striking them with sticks. The troops spread out again like a brand new flag.

—Onward! Onward, men! I positioned the platoon of snipers under a *chaparro* tree at one hundred fifty meters from the parapet. A new artillery burst made kindling of the tree that promptly fell down over our heads.

Now, all that was lacking was a supreme effort . . . The last one! . . . The cornets sounded the attack . . . sabers shone above the men's hats and . . .

Chapter Eighteen

—Onward! Onward! In the midst of infernal shouting, amid snorts of anger and choking, the entire line of men lifted up their bayonets—like the teeth of an upright comb—and threw themselves into the assault of redoubts and parapets after my sharpshooters.

We fell down mixed in with the enemy's slowest fighters and their wounded men. When the knives of the Mausers plunged into their fallen bodies it sounded like wineskins being ripped open.

It was necessary to take a breath in order to continue the chase, but anger and the desire for vengeance propelled the men along after the fugitives.

The spread-out town formed a collection of houses riddled with bullets and among them a swarm of women and children were fleeing, mixed in with the most spirited defenders who continued firing as they fled.

I proceeded along a planted field with an officer, the sharp shooters and a platoon of soldiers, harrying a platoon of fugitives with firepower.

I let my soldiers and those under my command rest in a nearby wood next to a ravine on the other side of the town.

Triumph made their eyes shine and perked up the expressions on their faces, which were still altered by the fight. In that corner of the woods we all breathed in life with mouthfuls of air and experienced a sensation of inexplicable wellbeing. To our right, soldiers from the column kept up their gunfire. In my judgment they had gone to intercept dispersed enemy forces from reaching the river.

We continued our march and guided by an *india* we caught up with, we emerged in a planted field in a position to hunt fugitives.

They began firing at us from the opposite bank and positioned as we were in the thicket of a dense jungle, disoriented momentarily by our march, I thought it was some dispersed platoon and I sent out soldiers to close the gap between us . . .

We landed right into a mudflat of the Zapote river, in the midst of a cove. Our presence was greeted with an almost circular heavy fire coming from the line of fortifications on the opposite bank. It was necessary to protect ourselves from inside the bend in the river and under a spray of bullets denser than a hailstorm, we tried to get out by holding onto the trunks of the jungle trees . . .

In the course of that flanking maneuver, a sharp, brutal blow took my breath away and made my entire body vibrate with pain. It made my muscles contract and forced me to close my eyes. I thought I saw small, glowing sparks through my eyelids. I was obliged to halt the section's march.

I was rigid, nailed to the spot, my left leg numb from the brutal blow. Through a tear in my trousers just below the groin I could see the torn skin at the edges of the wound. A stream of warm blood was spurting from the wound, moving down along my numb leg. I tried to put my handkerchief over the wound, but contact with the torn flesh burned like red-hot tinder. At that moment I was convinced that I had broken my leg and that I was upright only because a splinter of bone was still left. It was necessary to make an effort, to try to walk and to leave our compromised situation on the river in search of contact with the column. On our right, the fire coming from rifles and guns was decreasing, and in front the defenders of the other shore were aiming their shots at the forest. I made an effort and, masking my pain with angry cries, I took out my revolver, fearful of not being able to continue the march, and ordered an advance along the river, in the direction of the artillery fire.

My numb leg hesitated but didn't collapse and, amid stabbing pains, the hemorrhaging increased. I understood that it was going to be impossible for me to continue on foot for several hours and I ordered a retreat in order to go in search of contact with the column by taking a shortcut.

A painful march! . . . Lagging behind, I didn't want to tell anyone about my wound. My throat was dry and I was enduring the sharp pain, which was so deep and intense it was ripping out my guts.

When we were close to the column, crazed by pain, and debilitated during the march by my loss of blood, I felt my legs give way and, fearful that the bone was completely fractured, I called a halt and grabbed hold of the shoulders of one of the sharpshooters in the very moment when I was stunned by a hum that sounded like blood boiling in my arteries and, drenched by cold sweat brought on by the anguish that consumed me, I lost consciousness of space and light.

NOTE

1. The train serving a *sitio*, a territorial enclave that formed part of a *barangay* that was, in turn, a village, suburb, or other demarcated neighborhood. For information on the railway in the Philippines, see Republic of the Philippines, "PNR in Philippine History," n.d., http://www.pnr.gov.ph/about-contact-us/who-we-are/pnr-in-philippine-history/pnr-in-philippine-history.

Chapter Nineteen

They took me to rest in the improvised field hospital located om the bottom floor of a house in the town. While they searched for a stretcher, they put me on a pile of hay.

My two assistants, seated next to the horse's nosebag that I used for a headboard, were tireless in wiping off my sweat with their dirty handkerchiefs, in swatting away flies, or in fashioning screens from banana fronds to protect me from the sun.

Once the shock of the shot's impact had subsided, I began to feel more intense pain but, determined to conceal it as much as possible, I answered my companions' invariable question, "Are you in pain?" with a "No" that was as forceful as my pain.

One of the doctors came at last. As he prepared to examine my wound, he rolled up the sleeves of his military jacket and, with a resolution and gesture that brooked no reply, he took out some long scissors and proceeded to cut my trousers and underpants with circular cuts that produced a terrible sensation of coldness in the burning skin next to the wound.

When he finished cutting, the good *galeno* [Galen, doctor] told me, smiling, to "be strong" and introduced his index fingers into the wound. Shaking involuntarily, I felt that the piercing pain caused by the probe carried out by the doctor's fingernails was moving all the way up to my brain.

—It's nothing: no bigger than a buttonhole. A few days of rest and then out of here—the good doctor said, leaving me, in order to attend to the new wounded men who were being carried in.

Lying on the stretcher and wrapped up in blankets, I felt relatively good after the examination. Then I was overcome with thirst, a memory of the extreme thirst of recent days. They gave me cognac to drink and, somewhat comforted, I accepted a tin of pickled fish, which I devoured, mixing bits of bread with the fish bones. I felt better with each passing moment, and I even thought that the pain was letting up. A kind of languor spread through my entire body and, after that, a sudden sensation of warmth burned my temples and cheeks, little by little relaxing my entire body that, only moments before, was trembling with cold. I pulled the blankets up above my shoulders and, ordering the banana fronds taken away that were protecting my head, I let the sun, the splendid sun of that hot day that was singing a song of health and strength, to envelope me fully.

The celestial dome was clear and blue. From my observatory on the stretcher I was able to see the destroyed parapet, which we had assaulted hours before. Faces upturned, limbs torn apart and in strange positions, men, guns and lantacas were scattered on the wet, dug-up ground. I heard the deafening boom of the cannons, which momentarily blocked the incessant clatter of the artillery. They were still fighting there below and wounded men were coming in to take their places on the ground or on stretchers. Another man's pain sweetens one's own and the comforting sensation that moved up my body, wrapped in the warm folds of the blanket, increased at the sight of the horrors presented by the newly wounded men: arms broken at the joints, broken tibias, heads with gaps in the cranium, sunken chests enclosed in a breast-plate of mud and blood. The sun kissed all the unfortunate men on the ground equally, and the dead began to arrive next to the improvised hospital.

A pile began to take shape. Arms and legs ending in tapered fingers and yellowish fingernails dripping blood formed puddles on the ground. Their heads did not correspond to the posture of their bodies, and those dead men with glassy, questioning eyes, yellowish flesh and bloody necks, was a confused mass of flesh and wet clothes, torn and tangled by the action of the weight pressing down on it.

Little by little, the deafening noise of gunfire began to fade away. The cornets and bugles were clearly heard sounding the ceasefire and retreat.

As the soldiers returned from the frontline, they approached to examine the pile of dead and the row of wounded men. Our companions, still trembling and agitated by the danger they had just experienced, uttered words of consolation and sorrow.

—Good for the third Brigade! Good for the fifth, Good for Spain! The uninjured men cried out in joy, throwing their hats up in the air.

Spain! Spain! I recalled the trembling of the flag on board our ship, fluttering like a dying bird, and those flags, proud and gallant, that recently adorned the poop decks of the riverboats that were going to resupply the other column. I reviewed what had happened in the course of the day. Beyond the pile of our dead, the collapsed sand of the breached redoubt covered the destroyed bodies of its defenders.

Chapter Nineteen

The enemy fire had just stopped. The cornets, with the countersigns of the battalions, sounded the call to formation and, before forming, while they were still on the road, I heard a sudden irruption of soldiers who approached us dripping water from the river and shouting: Long live the wounded! Long live Spain! And a whiff of enthusiasm—the last one!—passed over the blouses of the pile of the dead, amidst gusts of wind agitated by the hats stained with yellow and blood which the living shook in their clenched fists, showing for lack of a better emblem, the red and gold of the flag of the fatherland. Long live Spain! One thousand times blessed is the nation whose sons, dripping mud and water, which made their overheated rifles smoke, returned from combat tremulous with ardor to aerate with their enthuasiastic breaths the sprawling pile of the dead, and to refresh the hot foreheads of the wounded men!

The cornets repeated the order to form on the double, and the soldiers disappeared waving their hats on high, splattered with blood and gold with the colors of the flag.

* * *

The Chinese brigade took charge of transporting the wounded men in stretchers covered with blankets.

Occupation forces remained in Pamplona and we returned to Parañaque passing through Las Piñas. Very close to this point the enemy, posted on the bridge over the Zapote River, jeopardized the rearguard and especially, the convoy of stretchers. For a moment, I feared that I was a sitting duck. My anxiety dissipated quickly because of the very sharp pain caused by the irregular pace of the frightened Chinese.

An odor of torn, palpitating flesh—less strong but *parejo* (like, as the *indios* say) the odor that in days past drifted in the air near the river and onto the shoulders of the men in the same brigade—passed over the convoy that was dripping blood all along the road.

During the march, vultures alighted on the tops of the trees and with an impatient gesture fluffed up their feathers with their sharp and yellow claws, looking from the depth of their *gachones* [charming], scheming eyes at the bloody wrappings on the stretchers.

After a rest and a medical examination performed on the road, we continued toward Parañaque, where at nightfall, the General in Chief came out to greet us.

We were transported to a raft fashioned from cane and, after long hours of anguish, of pain and waiting, a guerilla steamer came to tow us. Shortly before entering the sea in order to lead us to the bay, it collided with a weir and was on the point of sinking along with all its suffering baggage.

The terrible jolt prompted howls of distress, as well as protests and curses on the part of the uninjured men.

My good friend Argüelles, seated on the raft between two stretchers, tried to distract me, talking endlessly about unimportant facts and matters with floods of words that I confused in my painful, dejected condition with the sound of the foaming waves smashing against the sides of the raft.

The night was serene and warm, but the humidity of the bay and the first sign of fever brought an intense chill to my bones.

Awakened at times by fleeting relief from my pain, I listened to my good friend's words and the resounding complaints of the most gravely wounded men—all of it confused with the querulous groaning of the tow boat. Lying immobile on the stretcher, I saw the firmament studded with stars shining in the serene night with a compassionate and sorrowful twinkling.

Chapter Twenty

We were transported to the hospital beginning with our journey on the raft. It sailed along the river where small lanterns were swaying on the boats. Late at night we crossed into the walled city whose inhabitants were sleeping.

My stretcher was carried on the shoulders of four good friends. Upset by the motion, which despite being gentle caused me sharp pain, we traversed the walkway that skirts the length of the wall. Amidst weeping fronds of *ilang ilang* that opened up to the night the aromatic depths of its limp leaves we entered the Arroceros Road and soon after, the hospital.

Rings of guards, sanitary workers, and nurses accompanied the stretchers, illuminating the passage through a patio-parterre with lanterns in order to take us to a square, dark hall along whose four walls beds with mosquito netting were lined up.

It was the general hall destined for officers, which at the time, was empty. It began to fill up with the blood-soaked bodies of my companions in misfortune.

We were transported in turn amidst cries of pain that changed to deep sighs of satisfaction as soon as we were able to lie down between the sheets of the restful beds.

I slept for several hours, on edge because of the emotions I had experienced during the day. Pale morning light was entering through the opaque glass of the doors and windows when a sharp pain awakened me.

My good friend Argüelles remained at my side without having left the head of my bed for a single moment.

In the middle of the hall two Sisters of Charity, dressed in the starched fronts of their wimples and their blue garb, shook the long string of their rosaries with every movement as they carefully arranged broth, bottles of sherry, cups and siphons on a table.

The one who struck me as the youngest approached each bed and in a tone of plangent sweetness, exuding affectionate indulgence in her facial expressions—a face not lacking in charm—was offering a breakfast menu to each one of the wounded men.

She had words of consolation for everyone and, changing the kindly, compassionate look of her blue eyes to an expression of firmness and resolve, she managed to lift the spirits of the most downcast men.

Her name was Sister Joaquina. She responded with solicitude to all our demands, but it was necessary for us to first recognize the hierarchy that made her the general in chief, and for us to offer her our most submissive obedience.

She disappeared with her companion, Sister Ana, through one of the glass doors and the salon was sunk in a pained and dismayed silence, broken only by the choked groans of those men in pain, or the buzzing of the flies that, winging about the space, flew from mosquito net to mosquito net.

In the vast room painted a dark blue, the white, hermetically closed curtains around the empty beds were drawn back on those beds occupied by restless or immobile bodies. That allowed us to see bandaged and intensely pale heads or feet and hands wrapped in wadding through which we spied bits of flesh of a cadaver-like pallor.

The need to find a distraction from physical pain broke the silence and, despite faltering words, questions passed from one bed to another.

"Where did it hit, comrade?" Did it reach the bone?"

Pain and bursts of sympathy, choked up one man and made everyone quiet. Silence settled over the room, broken only by the buzzing of the mosquitos besieging the mosquito nets.

My good friend distracted me by speaking in the low, murmuring voice of a confessor and I, when pain permitted, opened up my clenched teeth and carried on the conversation in snatches.

When the Sisters returned with the task of distributing the breakfasts, the questions resumed and, after those questions, details of the assault and chase.

The wound hurt far more than under the immediate impact of the blow.

We all agreed that the pain of the first examination was worse than any that followed and, as we recalled that the doctor would not be long in coming to perform another examination, a disagreeable sensation passed from bed to bed obliging us to be quiet.

The good Sisters diligently doled out our biscuits, glasses of sherry, and cups of broth. Sister Joaquina again animated the dispirited conversation with her lively chatting when a bell announced the doctor's visit to the salon. The sanitary workers brought a folding table through the glass doors and propped it up in the center of the room. They arranged cases replete with sterilized

Chapter Twenty

instruments that shone to our terrified eyes with a brilliance that burned the imagination and the flesh. They were setting out in orderly fashion vials, irrigators, splints for a hand, a foot, a leg, an arm, and, in a corner of the table, big blue packages of absorbent cotton that made the room smell of that characteristic odor of phenol which our imagination associates with the idea of suffering. The room began to smell of misfortune.

The doctor appeared before long, attended by his students. He was of average height, with a rugged countenance and black eyes whose expression was bold and restless. He stood in the middle of the room with a self-assured attitude and a look of firmness about him.

—Gentlemen, good morning—, he said, turning his restless and penetrating eyes to the lines of beds.

Obligatory courtesy made us all greet him almost simultaneously

—Good morning, doctor—. And gritting our teeth in the hope of moving the pious hands of the doctor to examine us gently, each man emphasized his insignificance by pressing his body down under the bed sheets.

With professional aplomb he took off his white jacket and rolling up his sleeves he gave instructions to his sanitation workers and proceeded to dip his arms into a prepared solution in a container.

He hesitated for a moment glancing indecisively, not knowing where to begin . . .

The suffering men held their breaths and squeezed their bodies, immobile under the sheets so that they disappeared from the doctor's glance.

The good doctor decided on the bed closest to mine.

The students and the nurses formed an impenetrable wall so that we could not see the examination.

The men were submerged in a sepulchral silence . . . the doctor interrupted his quick and animated speech at times so that he could immerse himself in the task at hand . . . and then you had to hear the panting, agitated breathing of the patient's muffled crying . . . For God's sake, Doctor! . . . Ay! Mother! . . .

—I'm done, it's over— . . . the lively doctor was heard to say. He concealed his emotion by shouting for the phenol and cotton that the hesitant, overwhelmed sanitary workers were slow in handing to him.

The examinations continued and the auxiliary group surrounding the curtain-shrouded beds was leaving, carrying oilcloths and basins. My turn came, and in the midst of a convulsive trembling that made my lips tremble as they ventured a smile, I felt that my bedclothes were being removed.

The animated and noble glance of the doctor had a beneficent effect on me. I felt my spirits revive despite the contact of the oilcloth, which the sanitary workers spread over the sheets making me cold.

—A miraculous bullet, my son—, the doctor said, smiling, as he rolled up the bloody bandage covering my thigh in his right hand.

—Right next to the femoral artery—he said, turning to his students and, with a rapid movement he took two nickel probes from one of the boxes . . . I scratched the oilcloth, as I experienced a sudden jolt that made my body twitch . . . and after smelling the probe, the doctor turned to the nurses to recommend a diet for me. Then he proceeded to disinfect the wound. When I felt the contact of the cannula of the irrigator on my skin, I gritted my teeth to the point where I bit my handkerchief, and I abused the re . . . re . . . tonal scale in all imaginable keys. He concluded the examination by applying gauze to both openings of the wound and, after squeezing my arm affectionately, he went on to another bed not forgetting to repeat his recommendation for a strict diet and, smiling at me with a compassionate look, exclaiming by way of a goodbye: —One month at most!

The examinations resumed in the midst of weak complaints on the part of the men examined and the fearful silence of those who were waiting for their turn.

The good Sisters served biscuits and sherry, sweetening with their smiles and phrases the pressure of the doctor's hands.

The pain suffered by someone else was lessening the impression of one's own pain due to a phenomenon characteristic of egoism.

It was the turn of a wounded man whose voice we had not heard since he entered the salon.

The doctor tried to encourage him with his words, but confronted with the uselessness of his effort he had the nettings raised and ordered that he be given a potion which soon allowed us to hear the voice of the wounded man in between the kind words of the doctor who had just seated himself on the side of the bed.

—Well, my son, we have finally heard your voice!

—Ay! Doctor. For your mother's sake . . . tomorrow. Let me rest, My God! . . . The group of heads around the bed drew closer together . . . we could hear heartbreaking supplications, stifled sobs . . . laments that released the painful turmoil in his guts . . . Ah, no! Not there, not there, my God! . . . let me be for a moment . . . and after a sharp, piercing cry that reverberated in all the corners of the hall, we heard a hoarse, dry rattling in his throat that broke up the circle of nurses and led the doctor to look for a sedative on the table . . .

The silence was solemn. No one cried out in pain. The Sisters of Charity approached the group in concern . . . The man in pain moaned again and then uttered some words . . . His weakened voice seemed likely to end in a faint, and the doctor tried to rouse him between the cries and imprecations of a feigned harangue.

Chapter Twenty

—You must act like a man! Valor isn't only for when you are under fire! It's for here as well! We heard a resonant murmur. The doctor's words revived the patient's painful howls and, along with the bed's rough motion, which was creaking due to the patient's restlessness, we could hear the effort that produced two deep breaths.

—You must be strong! Be strong!

—But you are cruel, Doctor . . . Doctor, what are you doing! That's enough! Enough!

—Ay! It's over, my son! Some bones fell into a basin and, with a deep sigh of satisfaction, the doctor appeared from amongst the group of students and sanitation workers, his hands bloody, shaking his head sadly.

It was a matter of a nasty bullet that reduced the knee joint into splinters and powder.

The bandaging of the wound began, and while other healing measures were underway, anguished intermittent sobs weighed upon that bed of pain and misfortune leading Sister Joaquina and Sister Ana to pray and tell their beads since they had no words of consolation.

When he completed his ministrations in the hall, the doctor wiped his glasses carefully and, panting and smiling, after hastily grabbing his jacket, he saluted everyone, and ordering the table and the bloody basins removed, disappeared—a compassionate and proud man—through the door of opaque glass.

The hall was sunken in a painful silence, broken at times by alternating groans or deep sighs. A painful murmur of prayers or of anguish came from the patient's bed. The Sisters remained at his side.

An atmosphere of antiseptics and a strong odor of ether weighed on the air brightened with the day's radiant shining as it poured through the glass doors and windows. It lulled the senses, and obliged the swarm of mosquitos to take refuge on the ceiling and walls next to the doors.

Throughout the morning, slow, grave bells announced the visits of other parties. Friends came to visit us and their entrances and departures alternated with those of the assistants who discreetly half opened the doors to take or bring messages to their masters, or finally, install themselves at the heads of our beds. Outside when the door was opened, the light of a happy day with a serene and limpid sky poured in.

The hours of that day passed in an atmosphere of somnolence that immobilized our bodies beneath the hangings of our beds. At dinnertime, the Sisters took away the untouched plates and half an afternoon of drowsiness was snored away amidst anxious complaints. Odors from the kitchen brought back the irritating buzzing of the flies that contrasted in the quiet hall with the thin stream of fluid that fell drop by drop from an ad hoc apparatus on the destroyed knee joint of the wounded man.

I couldn't sleep. I closed my eyes but my senses, awakened to a pain so sharp that at times it cut off my breathing and prevented me from sleeping.

The buzzing of the mosquitos, the dripping of the apparatus and the sharp complaints of the suffering man peopled my imagination with phantasms when I closed my eyes. Now it was the formidable din of combat sustained in the middle of a blaze set by the enemy which was burning the bodies of the dead and wounded who could not be recovered; then it was our attack carried out as we walked on a combustible material that burned under the pressure of our feet and submerged our legs in ashes, obliging us to crawl. After limitless sacrifices we had to retreat and, going back over terrain we had already traversed, the flames burned our chests and shoulders. I visualized all the incidents that comprised the action. Further to the right lay the river. The burned soldiers went to submerge themselves in it under a horrendous barrage of firepower. The soldiers returned, their bodies dripping water, burned by flames at the side of the river. Like a passage of meteors they disappeared into the distance cheering the pile of charred dead and wounded men. I was thirsty, and when my good friend Argüelles was able to bring me back to reality, I felt my skin burning with fever along with the persistent, sharp pains caused by the probe.

Between periods of drowsiness the afternoon came to an end and with it came the insatiable thirst and pain that brought on intense, chaotic images. Shadows surrounded me and burning darts sparkled momentarily before piercing the skin of my legs. They came from far away, sent by an imperceptible *tic tac*, a sound similar to water dripping. At nightfall, a doctor came to see me who was with one of the battalions that had just arrived in Manila from the north of Luzón. An old friend of mine, he proceeded to revive me with his conversation and having resolved to alleviate the pain of my wound as he listened to my pleas for relief, he ordered a dose of morphine.

Several mortal moments passed before my assistant returned with the potion . . . I took one at first . . . and then up to three teaspoons of morphine in solution. At the third, I felt invaded by a lassitude that quieted the pain and then spread along my members a swelling voluptuousness that made my blood tingle and overwhelmed my senses with an ineffable and intoxicating ecstasy until I fell asleep amidst mysterious aromas and rhythmic music, under the rainbows of a soft, drowsy light that closed my eyelids.

I awoke close to dawn. The affected thigh felt like an alien attachment. It felt like I was the owner of a leg made of cork.

When I awoke again in the hall lit by the dim light of a small lantern placed in the center of the room, the white hangings of the beds stood out and through them the sound of painful, rasping breathing and the distinct dripping of the distilling apparatus over the bed of the wounded man. The bell at the

Chapter Twenty

door of the hospital that opened on the river rang with an impatient pealing. The Sisters silently crossed the hall, their rosaries clicking, and awakened the nurses sleeping with heads on their arms at the table in the center of the room.

—Wounded men arriving . . . wounded men from Silam.

It was the other column that was paying tribute to the insurrection.

In a short while, the bulky figures on stretchers came in giving voice to unintelligible moans. The wounded men had spent two days of painful marching along the lake and the river. They were very cold and their teeth chattered when they were taken off the stretchers. The invasion of new men not only filled the beds but also necessitated putting them on cushions on the floor.

The bell stopped ringing and the hall was submerged in the gloaming that the small lantern in the center of the room could not dissipate. It was changed for the moment by the complaints of the men who had been brought in and whose sighs and groans, as they began to find rest, started to subside in the shadows.

The dream populated with images appeared again before my eyes; my senses awakened to my real surroundings and, in the midst of the stench of the newly ripped open, bloody flesh, I went to sleep with a vision of my family, of my loved ones who, far away, beyond remote seas, awaited me, bursting with health and hope, in order to lovingly convey to me the life of the body and the mature peace of the spirit, heightened by the kiss of the breezes of my native land.

Chapter Twenty-One

The doctor arrived early for his visit the following morning . . .

As the pale light of day invaded the hall through the frosted windows, the wounded men who had arrived recently, turned and tossed impatiently in their beds.

The aides again placed the folding table of the day before in the center of the hall with its boxes, irrigators, and blue packets of absorbent cotton. The doctor, followed by his students and sanitary workers again formed diligent groups that surrounded the beds of their groaning patients. The Sisters of Charity resumed the task of encouraging the men who had been operated on.

It was late in the day when those of us who could be called old patients had our turn. When the doctor and his aides approached the bed of the man operated on the day before, they adjusted the apparatus designed to drip water and, after uttering some reassuring remarks, the doctor turned away with a contorted expression on his face.

There was no treatment scheduled for us. The doctor went from bed to bed, smiling, self-assured, checking the dressings and exchanging cheerful words with the patients.

He looked at my bandages and ordered my immediate transfer—along with the man with the fractured knee—to another hall. The head of the clinic decided that the officers' hall would serve from then on as the place to carry out medical treatments. Convalescent officers who still needed medical assistance began entering the hall. Men wounded in the head, figures who were densely pale and bent over who concealed scars on their chests under wadding, arms in slings, legs that swung like pendulums between crutches. Everything transpired in the bright light of a flood of sunshine that the doctor allowed to enter through one of the doors with frosted glass.

The group of students gathered around each one of the men being treated, a scene I ignored because I was nursing the pain that the Galen's hands had caused my suppurating flesh under the bandages.

Once, the doctor impatiently asked for a saw and was given a nickel-plated handsaw from the table. Through an opening in the group, I saw a bandaged arm in a shiny sling stick out and shortly after, I heard the teeth of the saw rubbing against something hard.

I trembled and forgot my pain to consider the other man's pain.

What were they doing? Sawing off an arm without anesthetic?

My friend Argüelles calmed me down: they were simply removing the plaster cast that protected a fracture. The pieces fell on the floor and I distinctly heard the patient say:

—Good. It's my arm and now it works.

When the doctor concluded his visit, he gave orders in a low voice to the Sisters. The hall was once again enveloped in silence, broken at times by the difficult and painful breathing of the men who had been operated on.

Argüelles, an old friend from my childhood, distracted me by recounting the vicissitudes of his first years of employment in the Archipelago. His life was mostly reduced to that experience since we separated. He disembarked in Manila when he was still a boy with a document confirming his employment and, after many years we met again, he, sick and without hope in the future, and I—according to him—with a promising life ahead of me and quite able to withstand all the pain I was experiencing at the present time.

My friend shared the pessimism of Sr. N. from Pampanga. He judged that the bloody and painful campaign would end in pacification for the moment, only to revive later and end our dominion over the Philippines.

He had no hopes of returning to Spain. He left as a very young boy, and during his years of residency in the country that made him a man, he learned through bitter experience to read in the book of destiny. He came to feel affection for his second country and he lost it in the end after successive troubles. He envisioned a very dark future for himself and for the country. One day, when they would finally face expulsion from the country, men who had left the best years of their lives in that land would return poor, poorer than when they left the mother country. No: the country was certainly not an ungrateful son who was seeking emancipation on reaching maturity. The country was leaving its mother for lack of maternal warmth, and the mother was resorting again to its old methods of discipline. It was not a matter of a year. Or five years. Not even a century. It amounted to three centuries of domination, of treating the country as an adoptive son, and in those three centuries not a single source of capital from the metropolis had been put at risk in those lands. Industry and commerce viewed those lands as untrustworthy recipients of the

Chapter Twenty-One

kind of credit extended to villagers. The government did not bother to favor the land with tariffs, and the paucity of commercial relations took the brutal imposition of the law to those lands. As if that were not enough to distance us from the metropolis—my friend Argüelles went on with passion—the damage done by politics in the country was greater. Parliament tired of calling the Archipelago our sweet son and, after discourses designed to seek employment for high functionaries charged with exploiting—half and half with governors and the opposition—the lucrative posts that eventually rendered barren the rich lodes of that wretched stepson, their lyrical speeches became abusive. In the end, after infinite pitiful credentials that rewarded labor and work with anemic returns, it turned out that elevated posts and the cancer of greed, fixed in the bowels of the land, was threatening to finish it off; greed was paying out pure gold for the outpourings of parliamentarian lyricism.

There was even more. Those countries, conquered with the cross and the sword, ended by surrendering to them, and out of sectarian pride Spain came to believe that religious power alone was sufficient to conquer those islands. The enterprise did well until Masonic power[1] at the beginning of the nineteenth century disputed the predominance of the religious orders in the metropolis. When the orders were defeated in the Peninsula, they sought to expand beyond the seas and once they were firmly entrenched, they defied the power of Masonry, and subsequently, they distrusted the army. Christ the Divine was enough to conquer those lands. And it would have been enough if the holy scene of the master casting out the merchants from the temple had not been repeated until it made a parable of the lashing and agitated the humble and needy every day, Masonry did not neglect its work and subject to living on spoils, once the Americas were lost it took on the task of feeding itself on the devastation of the political cancer. It lived like the crow and, like it, devoured the eyes that the dying body opened to faith.

The colony, removed from capital, from industry, from commerce, serving for a long time as the garbage dump of the dregs of the Peninsula or the means to satisfy political concupiscence fostered by the mother, living amidst the opposing sentiments of the sectarians, finally exploded and angrily decided to seek purity . . .

So much for the punishments. And unanimously, a commerce that had been stunted had recourse to politics, and politics, seeing its mother lode threatened, heeded the religious orders that asked for the help of the sword alongside the cross.

The governing directors of the nation saw the necessity of employing force to submit the ungrateful son and therefore sent more and more ships filled with troops, but it all obeyed a thought in the head that did not correspond to national sentiment. The ships were recruited in misery or they flew the flag of duty. Neither officers nor soldiers were fully cognizant of the problem they were setting out to resolve. In the judgment of everyone, those distant lands constituted a political prebend where the evil men would be aggrandized and the good men would perish. The problem had nothing to do with the central Castilian plateau where the *indianos*[2] never came; nevertheless, as in Cuba, the soldiers were recruited from the central plateau because recruitment kept pace with poverty . . .

When he reached this point, indignation caused my good friend's eyes to open wide, and his very white, freckled complexion reddened with the blood that flowed to his face . . .

Horrible! In his opinion there was nothing more horrible than to undertake a war without enthusiasm. And those men who entered the hospital in flocks could not feel the enthusiasm necessary for a long campaign. They would certainly feel patriotic ardor in combat spurred on by the colors of the flag, but alas! that was not enough without having another sentiment in one's heart. The flag, splattered and reddened in battles would take on the uniform color of blood. And, at the sight of blood the color yellow would only be the color of sterility. What was the purpose of that struggle? What was being preserved? What was being promised in the long run? . . . Yellowness and blood. The color of the dead was the color of the flag and the flag represented the cause marvelously well. Horrible! Horrible! In the midst of the uselessness of the effort, he was proud, for he had just enlisted in a battalion of volunteers, and he saw that the soldiers were fighting with the enthusiasm of previous times. He evoked the image I communicated to him of troops that had been burned, coming out of the river, and then going to greet the wounded men, and amidst *vivas*, aerating the piles of dead men with the breeze of their hats waved in salutation.

Horrible! Horrible! All that effort at the service of a wretched industry, a weak commerce and a disastrous politics would end in a flood of blood. It was already flowing into the hospital in torrents . . .

My friend grew silent and shortly after, the bell on the door that opened onto the river signaled the arrival of new barges with wounded men.

The Sisters mobilized the nurses and through them we found out that there had been a bloody action in the Zapote and that among the wounded soldiers and officers was the corpse of the heroic colonel Albert . . .

The news upset the hall. Everyone there imagined the figure of the gallant coronel. A solemn silence followed. The incessant dripping at the bed of the man wounded in the knee was interrupted by his agitated tossing and turning. He murmured between clenched teeth:

—Albert! Albert!

It was necessary to put the beds closer together in order to fit in more beds.

Chapter Twenty-One

My friend's long speech and his reasoning produced deep unrest in my spirit together with the news of Albert's death.

An odor that I took for a bad omen came from my bed and from the bed of the man whose knee was operated on.

Sister Joaquina came by, affectionate and smiling, to tell us that they were going to transfer us to open up new room for more wounded men and, so that isolated in other rooms, we might rest. I was alarmed at the possibility of gangrene setting in and despite the calming words of Argüelles, when the hour for the transfer arrived and nurses lifted my bed on their shoulders, it was enough to see the pained goodbyes of my fellow wounded men to confirm my fear.

They carefully removed the apparatus of the man who had been operated on and behind his bed they carried mine, making us traverse the length of the patio of palms that I saw covered in shadows when I arrived.

I anxiously breathed in the first whiffs of the sun-warmed air as we went down the staircase. The opaque glass door that opened onto the general hall filled with beds and stretchers closed behind the head of my bed.

As we passed through the patio-parterre I spied opposite us innumerable stretchers that were transporting wounded men from the barges to the halls for soldiers.

The assistant at my side who came to take a look, said to me, "Many men from the company are coming in, *señorito*."

—From the company?

I recalled Argüelles' words, the enthusiasm of my soldiers, and the tribute of blood that we paid in the first assault. A strong effort was not enough. Many efforts were needed and time would drown enthusiasm in blood, leading all the soldiers to the enervating and crushing interpretation of the red and yellow colors of the flag: red, the color of blood; and yellow, the color of sterility.

NOTES

1. Freemasonry in the Philippines was short-lived during the pre-revolutionary and revolutionary period. The first lodge organized in the Philippines to admit Filipinos dates from 1890. The official organ of the Filipino masons in Spain stated the objectives of the organization: "Masonry will exist as long as there is tyranny, for Masonry is but an organized protest of the oppressed. And tyranny will prevail in the Philippines as long as the government remains in the hands of the friars at the service of their interests. For that reason, tyranny in the Philippines is synonymous with oligarchy of the friars, and to fight against tyranny is to fight the friars." *La Solidaridad*, official organ of the Filipino masons in Spain (quoted in *La Solidaridad*, "History of

Philippine Masonry," *Philippine Center for Masonic Studies*. n.p., http://www.phil ippinemasonry.org/philippine-masonry-from-barcelona-to-manila-1889-1896.html).

The discovery of the Katipunan in 1896 led the Spanish government to ban Masonry in the Archipelago, since it considered Masonry to be the source of insurrectionist ideology. In 1897 Francisco Foradada, S.J., author of *La Soberanía de España en Filipinas, Opúsculo de Actualidad* (Barcelona: Henrich y Compañía, 1897), wrote that: "Thus it is clear that Philippine *filibusterismo* [subversion] is not the offspring of the law, of morality or of justice, but rather of masonry, the enemy of God and of all that is good, just and holy" (quoted in Philippine Center for Masonic Studies, n.p., "The Katipunan and Masonry: 'The Revolution.'"). See also Teodoro A. Agoncillo, *Revolt of the Masses: The Story of Bonifacio and the Katipunan* (Quezon City: University of the Philippines, 1956); and Teodoro M. Kawlaw, *La Revolución Filipina / The Philippine Revolution* (Manila: Manila Book Co., [1925]).

2. The term *Indianos* was used to refer to Spaniards who lived and worked in Cuba or in other former Spanish possessions in the New World, then returned enriched to the motherland. They were often satirized for their social pretensions by contemporary novelists such as José María Pereda. Ricardo Burguete's reference to recruitment to military service keeping pace with poverty alludes to the law of 1896 on military conscription. Exemption from service on the Peninsula was permitted upon payment of 1,500 *pesetas*. Exemption from service outside the Peninsula was granted upon payment of 2,000 *pesetas* (Elena Hernández Sandoica and María Fernanda Mancebo, "Higiene y sociedad en la Guerra de Cuba (1895–1898): Notas sobre soldados y proletarios," *Estudios de Historia Social* 5–6 [1978]: 361–84, at 364). The central plateau was a poor region that produced many conscripts precisely because of its poverty. According to the Dirección General de Agricultura, in the Peninsula as a whole in 1903 the income for a rural family of five subsisting on a diet of bread, oil, garbanzos and dried fish was minimally 1.80 *pesetas* per day (Fernando Puell de la Villa, F. *El soldado desconocido, De la leva a la "mili" (1700–1912)* [Madrid: Editorial Biblioteca Nueva, 1996], 216).

Chapter Twenty-Two

They took me down a corridor whose rooms opened on the left and right. My bed was placed in a small room. The rooms were separated by thin partition walls that shook with the coughing of patients on either side along with the sound of their breathing.

Fear of gangrene was not an idle worry on my part. The discomfort and anxiety I experienced on the first night of my move and the doctor's painful examination the following day lent material proof to my reasonable apprehension. My neighbor was in a sorry state and in the judgment of a consultation held among several doctors, it was necessary to amputate his leg that afternoon.

I tossed and turned in the bed and was made more uncomfortable by the heat at midday in the small room and the oven-like temperature at the hour of the siesta. The sun streamed through the only open window, making the varnish sweat and heating the knots in the wood. A strong odor of cooking came from the end of the corridor and, as it spread though the rooms, it brought a greasy, annoying swarm of flies that flew about the fringes of the mosquito netting.

Sister Teresa, the new sister, prayed in an unoccupied room next to mine.

My friend Argüelles, absent for a few hours, would not be long in coming back and at the foot of my bed the nurse's little cap and Chinese shirt, as he called them, were ready for him . . .

I began to distract myself from my sharp pains and solitude by recalling long lost memories. And captivated, despite severe cramps, by the hypnotic power of the past, I began to relax in the recollection of times gone by when an unusual movement in the corridor caught my attention. My assistant came to tell me that my neighbor was being taken to the amputation chamber and doctors were coming in advance to administer chloroform. I distinctly heard the murmur of many voices speaking energetically and convincingly. Then supplications, sobbing and, after the gasping for breath of a body turning about in the bed, we heard inarticulate phrases, choked cries and finally, energetic orders communicated in low voices. It wasn't long before we heard along the corridor the dragging of feet and brushing against the walls produced by the arms of a stretcher. I managed to see the group, followed by the doctors who carried under blankets the immobilized body of the man who had been given chloroform.

Barely half an hour later, a nurse appeared carrying a bucket containing a leg, as yellow as wax, dripping blood, and wrapped in a piece of sheet.

Argüelles' arrival coincided with the return of the stretcher that caused the bodies of the carriers to brush against the walls along the length of the corridor. They told me that the stretcher held the body of the unfortunate man who, without coming to as yet from his anesthetic, had just had his leg amputated high up on the thigh, severed almost at the trunk.

I could not sleep that night, not even by abusing the bromide I was given.

Early in the morning the man whose leg had been amputated regained consciousness with heartrending cries.

The nurses in attendance, together with the Sister, gave him a sedative that quieted the sharp explosions of pain and led to whimpering, weak groans. Sometimes the patient spat out blasphemies and supplications, railing no longer against fate but against the implacable pain.

—But, my God, what is happening? My foot hurts; the left foot, the foot that's gone!

I recalled the tortures Silvio Pellico[1] described. This wretched man complained in the same way and pleaded for the relief of his poor body whose torn flesh was suffering misery and pain.

The sight of that bucket and that yellowish leg passed before my eyes; dead and unfeeling flesh that, buried or thrown into the river by then, tormented—a very common phenomenon—the abandoned body of the living man.

NOTE

1. Pellico (1789–1854) was the author of an account of his imprisonment for subversion by the Austrian police in the fortress of Speilberg in Moravia. See *My Ten Years Imprisonment*, trans. Thomas Roscoe. Project Gutenberg, 2000.

Chapter Twenty-Three

The days and nights came and went. I endured that period of time helped by my good friend who, seated at the head of my bed, left it only to rest at night or in order to attend to necessary matters during the day.

The day of my recovery was drawing near, but in the meantime a multitude of emotions replaced my bodily pains.

The nearby rooms of the long corridor were filling up as the operations of the Sungay column continued to advance and, judging by the frequent medical discharges in the hospital, we were keeping abreast of the fighting.

The bell announcing the arrival of bloody barges on the river was not still for a moment.

New victims arrived every day and attacks happened every day.

Each convoy of flesh implied a day's effort and by such efforts alone the path was cleared and the flag that waved at the surge of the advancing troops was kept upright.

Spain! Spain! All day long, soldiers coming from the Piñas and the advance troops of the Zapote, brought—along with news of the most recent operations—bursts of enthusiasm and an air of health and risk that enlivened the atmosphere around the beds heavy with iodoform, grief and misfortune.

At nightfall and throughout the nocturnal silence, the wounded men's imaginations, fed by madness-inducing deliriums or leaden periods of wakefulness, led them to cry out enthusiastically Spain! Spain! Cries that were weak at times and sometimes robust in response to the cry "Who goes there?" of the sentinels posted on the banks of the river.

My friend Argüelles did not appear one afternoon and evening and, coinciding with the hours of his usual arrival, an unusual movement caused a commotion among the sanitary workers and nurses. And after that came an order in the name of the official on watch for my assistants to arm themselves in order to reinforce the patrols charged with defending the building.

From the sergeant charged with informing me of the request, I learned that on that very morning an indigenous force of carabineers had risen up and that in the outer neighborhoods numerous groups affiliated with the Katipunan supported the movement. Denunciations had just led to the arrest of some of the staff in the hospital. In the morning hours there was no information about the insurrectionary movement because volunteers and troops were fighting the uprising in the streets.

I remained alone, completely alone in my room-cell and through the glass of my half-open window a sleepy, sad afternoon unrolled, broken by the passage of the patrols that were going to reinforce the cordoned-off area of the river or the exterior doors that were in a potentially vulnerable position.

Sunk in the solitude of the room and my abandonment, at nightfall I thought I heard distant firing that made a humming noise in my pillow clearly different from the sounds I heard from my tossing and turning . . .

Night fell and Sister Ana did not talk me out of my doubts with her customary indifference.

It was after midnight when the relief guards sent back my assistants and through them I heard news gleaned in the outpost.

The insurrection had been defeated on the streets, but there were many casualties on both sides.

Half of the indigenous nurses and interns in the Faculty of Medicine were taken prisoner when it was verified that they were forging a plot to kill off the wounded patients and set fire to the hospital when the rebellion got underway.

All morning long I heard the crossing of the patrols beneath my window alternating with the "alerts" of the sentinels who were securing the outside of the building.

My friend's nurse's garb was at the foot of my bed. I thought that since he was affiliated with a volunteer guerrilla group, he was perhaps fighting against the dispersed members of the uprising.

Very early in the morning, I managed to get to sleep for a short time. I was awakened by the hustle and bustle of the daily medical examination.

The good doctor came to my bed and while he took my pulse as I was looking about for my good friend, he ordered that I be given a bromide.

He didn't examine my bandages and sitting down at the foot of my bed, he said in a tremulous, affectionate voice:

—I don't think that I lack courage to give you a distressing piece of news: your friend Argüelles was gravely wounded in combat with the insurrectionists and there is no hope of saving him.

The gravity of the fatal, irreparable calamity brought tears to my eyes.

Chapter Twenty-Three

—Is he dead?

—Yes, dead. A bullet to the head. But you have to master your grief, Come now! You must prepare to fortify your spirit . . .

I swallowed the bitter news. The abnegation of my good friend, of my good nurse, during my stay in the hospital passed through my mind and, at the same time I saw in my mind's eye his brotherly, affectionate face in the clothing that was at the foot of my bed, awaiting the warmth of its owner.

His jacket fell to the floor when a sanitation worker brushed by it and I thought of the fall of my good friend, detached from life like a bloody rag flung down on the street.

—It's necessary to be strong, the doctor repeated. Physical strength is not enough; we must also have moral strength and, with its help, overcome everything. I struggle too, my son. And I suffer afflictions of body and soul. I would like to have one hundred lives to treat my sick men and one hundred hands to help them . . . I struggle tooth and nail against death . . . in exchange for my health I fight for another man's health and, nevertheless, death, fighting against my efforts carries them off. One cannot fight against one's destiny; it is necessary to succumb to its demands . . . It is less distressing when it comes all at once and takes a life, but how cruel it is when it offers hope, when it lends courage for the fight and defies what is inevitable with a glimmer of support, of weakness on the part of the enemy!. . . I am made to fight and I end up declaring myself conquered without ever capitulating. You know how hard I tried with the last man whose leg was amputated. Yet, in the end he died and he was taken away from here secretly. I fought for him more than words can say, I came to treat him at unusual hours, I fought against my fatigue, I fought death tirelessly and death came. Last night in the general hall another man died for whom I held out hope based on my care. A vain determination in both of us . . . But I don't falter. I have other patients, and, with the help of my health and life I will restore their health and let them live . . . It is necessary to overcome misfortune and be strong. You are heroic in the trenches, I am heroic here, next to the beds of my patients. The mission is glorious in both instances. You restore honor and I restore life. There is heroism there and heroism here: all sacrifice of life for another's benefit is heroic.

I listened to the doctor and was consoled and more in conformity with the news of my friend's death. I saw in the doctor's face the ravages caused by his active life. His abnegation and his work elicited lively recognition and gratitude in his patients. From the day of his first visit, one could see the dull pallor of fatigue in the doctor's face, and through the lens of his glasses a violet oval rimmed the lively black eyes of . . . (I was on the verge of being indiscreet).

He left me with a hearty handshake and I heard him exclaim as he walked along the corridor:

—There are no procedures today.

The doctor received cheerful greetings from all the rooms, along with sighs of satisfaction from patients whose painful flesh would enjoy a reprieve.

When the visit was over, my thoughts returned to my poor friend who took leave of me the day before with his customary "I'll see you later." I recalled his pessimism and I realized that his prophecies were beginning to be fulfilled: the insurrection was growing and threatening to ignite the entire population of the Archipelago . . . He had no hope of returning to Spain or even of seeing the sterility of the war effort.

I remembered the afternoon when we were riding in a coach along the roadways and he pointed out the great number of *bahais* in the outer neighborhoods. There, there the focus of the revolt was anchored, and from there would come the formidable surge of violence.

The death of my friend at a crossroad—one of those places that he had pointed out—put a sad seal of truth on the rest of his assertions.

All morning men wounded the previous afternoon were entering the hospital. At midday a sad and measured ringing of the bell, followed by a dragging of feet—a sound I recognized—crossed through the patio, reminding me that they were going to administer the viaticum to the most gravely ill men. For a moment a line of artificial light illumined the quadrangular frame of the window and, during the afternoon the wood, which was exposed to the sun, began to sweat tears of resin from the knots that looked at me fixedly, like bloody pupils.

Chapter Twenty-Four

One day, after one and a half months of immobility confined to my bed, the doctor authorized me to get up. They brought me some brand new crutches that I learned my solicitous and affectionate friend—lost forever—had ordered in advance in his eagerness to see me walking so as to realize our projects for a happy and tranquil convalescence in an estate he had rented.

Hanging on the crutches without succeeding in taking a step, I went out with the help of my assistants to the central patio where, at the time, other wounded men and sick patients were breathing in the fragrant morning air.

They put me in a *dormilona* [long chair] made of wicker and, propped up with pillows, I ordered them to leave the tantalizing crutches next to the top of the chair.

With delight I breathed in deeply the air warmed by the sun and the scents given off by the aromatic plants of the parterre.

The one-story hospital had a radial system of galleries and halls that ended in staircases protected by overhangs of wood and zinc. Slender palm trees, attractive bushes and multicolored plants rose up in the small central plaza, which was covered in sand along the length of its maze of flowerbeds.

Stretched out in the chair and little more than a hand span above the stone flagged ground, I saw a bit of clear and serene blue sky. In the distance the firmament outlined the graceful silhouettes of trees whose leaves, ruffled by the breeze, sang joyfully, stirred by the puffs of sweetness emanating from the diaphanous, blue cloudscape.

I answered the questions of my comrades and entered into the general conversation of the men who, forming a ring and placed in capricious postures, took care to avoid rubbing the painful part of their bodies against the chair when they moved.

Padded shoulders and chests bulging with bandages: heads and faces hidden by turbans of cotton wool; arms sheathed in patent leather halters; hands and feet in splints, wooden supports that appeared under bundled-up wrappings—such was the appearance of the group of officers who were chatting together.

On the opposite side of the parterre in the wing of the building destined for the infirmary of the troops, the convalescent men dressed in the robes of invalids, chatted in groups or walked about supported by the arms of nurses or hanging on crutches.

I spent a long time looking at a soldier whose leg had been amputated taking his first steps on crutches and then taking his first steps unassisted with crutches along the rough, sanded avenues in the garden.

I believed that that agility was the result of a prodigious ability.

Until then I hadn't stopped to consider the difficult maneuvers involved in maintaining one's balance while on crutches.

Ah! How long would it be until I might learn how to do it!

Chapter Twenty-Five

After a few days and some risky attempts, I succeeded by dint of perseverance in learning how to use crutches. And when, one perfumed and melancholy afternoon, I managed to walk across the parterre, I felt a surge of happiness and a sudden emotion that made me stop next to a clump of palm trees and hide my face bathed in tears.

I was unable to stifle my sobs for a long time. I didn't know then and I don't know now why I was crying. But without knowing why, tears flowed abundantly down my cheeks and shook my body with an ineffable sensation of relief.

I was crying because I was mobile again . . . I was crying because of traumatic hysteria, according to my doctor. But no: that is not a sufficient explanation. I was crying over something more than that, and I felt my body weaken in a surrender to tender feelings that almost caused me to sink to the ground in the midst of the perfumed and melancholy afternoon.

When the crisis passed, I straightened my body and continued to head for the stairway that led to the general hall for wounded soldiers. The yellow and black van that carried dead men to the morgue or the amphitheater passed by very close to me.

I ascended the stairway on the arms of nurses and walked along the lines of beds in the hall in search of familiar faces among the soldiers.

Some men were sitting up bolstered by pillows. Others were stretched out like dead bodies; or they were turning over restlessly under the sheets, shaken by pain. All the faces of the sick men, which were as yellow as wax, contrasted with the healthy faces of the nurses and sanitary workers who were giving medicines to the wounded men, hastening to respond to their calls, or forming changeable groups that were dressing the convalescing men or helping them to take their first steps.

On some empty beds that had just been cleared, a little tablet inscribed with the word "deceased" replaced a small plaque with a number on it, which lent to the pile of pallets and pillows gathered at the head of the bed the suggestion of a sensation of freezing, of humidity, of cold.

I went along the line of beds greeting and receiving the affectionate congratulations of some of my soldiers. On one of the beds, a white linen sheet covered the rigid body that had just expired. On the next bed, a wounded man moved his eyes with an expression of infinite anguish and looked unceasingly at the folds of the sheet that revealed the rigidity of the protuberant parts of the livid, freezing body.

I turned to go out after restoring hopes for a speedy recovery in the soldiers from my company. Very close to the door, inundated in the light of a dying twilight and open to perfumed breezes that freshened the heavy odor of iodoform and phenol, a nurse approached leading a blind soldier who extended his arms toward me in the void and called out to me indistinctly:

—Captain! My captain!

I looked at the unfortunate man and recalled that on the day of the attack he took a bullet that passed across his forehead and left him alive miraculously, emptying his eyes . . .

I grasped him affectionately by the arm and at the sound of my voice I felt him tremble and, blinking painfully, his face took on a sad expression:

—I can't see any more, my captain. I can't see but I hear your voice; it's fine now. I know that you are using crutches because I can hear them. What a pity, my captain, not to be able to see familiar faces from the past. Will you heal completely?

—Yes, my son, may God bless you, I shall come back to see you. And I left there in anguish at the plight of the poor blind man.

The following morning in the hospital, we heard about a new and hotly contested combat involving the Sungay column.

When the doctor arrived to examine me, he announced that on the following day I would be transported to the convent of the Jesuit Fathers. I learned that the different communities would divide up the convalescent men in order to free the hospital rooms for new arrivals of wounded men.

I left the hospital after an early morning visit to the general hall of officers, the hall for soldiers, and to take leave of the Sisters.

I said goodbye to my bed and the little room and went out to take a coach to the convent. I went down the stairs by myself supported by the crutches and feeling my leg sway like a pendulum.

When the vehicle left the doors of the hospital to which I bade an affectionate, emotional farewell, the bell of the door rang announcing the presence of the river launches.

Chapter Twenty-Five

On a splendid morning, drawn by a horse at a walking gait, the coach traversed the Arroceros Road and followed the river leaving the Puente de España on the right for entry to the gates of the walled city. Breathing in mouthfuls of air seemed to do my lungs good, making the blood in my veins hum and warming my face.

It seemed to me that I was entering another world. The world of the fortunate, and it gave me pleasure to see people on the left and right walking about fresh and agile.

A landau with a bouquet of pretty European women passed by my side en route to the roadway. The sight of the women's colored parasols, which served as a covering, was lost in the distance amidst clouds of dust that intermingled with an overflowing froth of tatting and lace.

I breathed in the odor of healthy, rosy flesh and trembling, I entered Old Manila to the ringing of bells that seemed to me to be a cheerful harbinger of the serenity and peace of the refuge I was invited to share.

Chapter Twenty-Six

Once in the convent, I was lodged in a pleasant cell whose windows opened onto a lane.

The dominant color of the bed I was to sleep in was ermine white. Its extreme narrowness continuously reminded the body and spirit of the idea of chastity and celibacy, making any sinful dreams impossible on a cot which scarcely provided room to support oneself on the sides of the bed so as to turn over.

A table with devotional material, straight-backed chairs, a lounging chair on one side, and pictures illustrating miraculous Biblical stories completed the furnishings of the room which, without any luxury whatsoever, breathed blessed quietude, solemn retreat, and mysterious unction.

The good Fathers, concerned about my comfort and desires, frequently asked about my wishes, and they carried on spirited conversations on the war, providing me continuously with whatever newspapers and sources of news contained accounts of operations.

The Community's severe rules allowed the Fathers few hours of leisure. During that time we convalescent patients hurried to the visitors hall, next to a wide, sunny corridor that looked out to the sea and from which one could see the coasts of Cavite.

Moved by feverish interest and aided by the powerful telescopes that the Fathers brought from the observatory, we were able to follow the operations of the Sungay column every day. The Community rejoiced at each triumph of our arms and at the sight of our flags waving on the towers of the enemy towns after our successful attacks, visible through the powerful telescopes. News of each triumph arrived at the convent almost as soon as it arrived in the official centers.

A permanent guard manned by the Brothers to announce the arrival of news was set up, and when news was announced through the ringing of bells, on occasion it interrupted religious conversations when they had just begun.

Except for these opportunities or during the rest time in the afternoons, the Community disappeared in order to teach their numerous students or to enter the open cells along the wide passageways with their sumptuous wooden floors. The convent palace consisted of four adjoined sections of the building that ringed a patio designed for the gymnasium and recreation of the live-in students.

Students, classes, libraries, studies, and museums occupied two wings of the convent and the other two were meant for the use of the Fathers, among whose cells—the best—they set aside for the ill.

We did not eat in the general refectory. Two Brothers served us in a sunny room that opened onto the street that continually conveyed the mundane sounds of the outside world to us.

They served abundant fortified wine, and well-seasoned food at our table, which was not lacking in distinction and was adorned on a daily basis with fragrant flower arrangements.

The good Brothers, withdrawing into temporary states of discreet distraction, seemed quite unaware of the snippets of our conversations that at times crossed a line, or they warmly joined our discussions on the war, when—letting lie references to opoponax[1] and warm discussions of various embodiments of the descendants of Eve, we returned to the unending topic of our profession and the war.

When the prior and the Fathers left the refectory, they joined us in our after dinner conversations, asking: "Did our patients eat well?"

When dessert arrived in the dining room the open happiness of convalescents returning to life in the peace of the cloister predominated at the table.

The animated faces of the Fathers, who exuded health and strength, seemed to affect us in the atmosphere of retreat and peace that filled the halls and rooms in the convent.

News of the latest act of heroism performed in the daily attacks was the obligatory topic of the most recent conversation . . . The Fathers were fond of heroes. They had some in their ranks and at times they pointed them out in the pictures on the dining room walls . . .

The pictures were not at all bad. One of them represented a shipwreck: the crew had just crowded into the launches as their last hope when a Father of the Company, kneeling on the deck during the onslaught of gigantic waves, disappeared, refusing to follow the other men so that his last prayers and sacrifice would serve as an act of redemption that would save the shipwrecked men crowded into the launches. Another picture represented the martyrdom of a Father dressed like an Indian fakir amongst implacable, ferocious tribes. In another picture, a cannibal feast was being prepared. A tribe of negroes was getting ready to roast an old man alive whose arms, fastened behind his back, left his hands free enough to lift a crucifix to his lips which he kissed between prayers . . . Their names were Friar Domenech . . . Friar Juan. I don't remember their names. I don't believe that the Community knew them for certain. They were anonymous heroes whose exemplary sacrifices provided a lesson to everyone, repeated and enhanced by the halo of their very lack of fame. They died one day, at a given hour—the date and the moment do not matter—and in the obscurity of their sacrifice they went on to live a posthumous life in those pictures lining the walls of that sunny dining room, the only room in the house where we were aware of the swirl of the happy, mundane life of the world outside.

The community withdrew early in the evening and arose at dawn with the happy call to matins followed shortly by the ringing of the bell for first mass, which the Fathers heard in the adjacent church that was connected to the Palace convent.

In the days that followed, I grew accustomed to the ambient stillness, which calmed the body and spirit more effectively than doses of sedatives.

Under streams of sunlight filtered through the green blinds of my room, I invariably awoke when day broke to the happy ringing of bells, the plaintive, penetrating sound of the church organs that made my flesh tingle with impulses of peaceful and vigorous life.

My wound was healing. The good doctor did not abandon us for a single day. Each time I saw him, the dark, olive-colored circles [*pisadas*] under his eyes, caused by fatigue and exhaustion, became more noticeable on his pale face.

I traversed the length of the corridors, performing prodigies with my crutches; I chatted with the rest of my companions or I went to the visitors salon to seek distraction by gazing at the broad expanse of water or the lush forest of the distant enemy coast.

The Fathers walked silently along the corridors, carrying their rosaries and a prayer book and then, after greeting us with an inclination of their heads, they disappeared in their black habits into the openings in the wall which led to the cells.

One morning the customary routine of the convent was changed for an entire day. It was the day when Imus[2] was taken.

Imus was the key to the insurrection for everyone. For a long time the enemy had accumulated such defenses and such hopes that defeating them would mean the end of the war. From very early in the morning we installed ourselves in the visitors salon taking turns looking through the telescopes that focused on the cupola and church tower of the enemy town.

The forest, which blocked our view of the estate house, was spread out like the sea so that it was difficult to follow the column's progress. In mid-morning a small cloud of smoke that was moving above the tops of the trees and which we knew from previous attacks was an indication of a battle, settled over the outskirts of the town. The small cloud did not advance resolutely as on other occasions. It was stationary and, after making us impatient during many hours of observation, we heard the bell signaling mid day.

Steam launches moved over the smooth surface of the sea, carrying and communicating orders to the squadron, which, anchored off the coast of Cavite, opened fire on the enemy towns close to the coast.

During the meal, we spoke of nothing but the outcome of the fight.

Uncertainty, which is always cautious, exaggerated the insuperable defenses of the enemy. And fear of a misfortune after the rapid succession of triumphs was visible on everyone's face, prompting the spirited fathers to exclaim: "It is strange that the smoke isn't moving away as usual."

We returned to the windows that served as our observatory. Apprehension swept hope away and made us think that the circle of smoke was moving away more and more beyond the town's boundary. The afternoon drew on and with great anxiety given the clear atmosphere, we saw the column of smoke fade or move far away. Finally the coming and going ceased and the smoke began to move off as if swept away by the wind, first for a small distance, then another, until it disappeared within the confines of the forest. Everyone's spirits plunged in dismay and our astonished eyes, opened extremely wide, peering into the distance, could not find a pretext to reject that reality. It was moving: the smoke was clearing. There was no doubt that they were retreating. At what cost? What horrible disaster was rolling back our soldiers as if they were being swept away by storm winds? There was no hope. We put down the telescopes that focused silently on the church tower of Imus, about to be covered by the shadows of the afternoon that for all of us was beginning to change in the midst of a tragic silence.

The Brother who served as a guard moved the telescope and answered our glances with negative signs: "The smoke was moving off."

Then, as he was cleaning the reticle with his habit, he shouted: "The flag, the flag!"

The commotion was so violent for all of us that we rushed to the telescopes and, when the second observer saw the same thing, a unanimous salvo of applause burst out. Spain! Spain! It was true. On the top of the tower the country's red and yellow flag was gallantly waving. Red with the blood its sons shed to save it, yellow with the yellowish insignia of glory. I stayed glued to the telescope for a long time whose glass was steamed up by the tearful mist of enthusiasm. In the end, ours was the triumph and the glorious emblem, pointing toward the West, shaken by a strong breeze, which a bit earlier scattered the clouds of smoke, was vibrating tremulously in space, splattered with blood and gold.

Coinciding with reality and our joy, all the bells in the parishes unexpectedly began to ring. The news had been sent to everyone and shortly, explosions of rockets and flares scratched the open skies breaking the tragic silence of the day which in turn, seemed to us to decline smiling among the shadows, there in the distance on the vast surface of the sea.

Early in the evening emissaries came to communicate news to the convent. Manila was decorated with hangings on balconies. Rockets and flares were blasting fire into space and musicians had orders to circulate in the central neighborhoods to animate the crowds and spread the joy.

We had conquered the key to the insurrection, but only through streams of blood. The first news we received estimated our casualties to be nine hundred to one thousand men.

Night fell. After dining and after lively toasts, I retired to my rooms, undone by the day's emotions that were making the scars of my wound itch.

Through the half-open window the joyful ringing of the bells and the bursts of firecrackers and rockets mixed with distant music and shouts. A *"viva España"* tremulous, weak and then louder reached my ears, like the shout I heard in the journey across the sea. I remembered the flag folded on the "Alfonso XIII," palpitating weakly like a dying creature; later on, the flag swollen on the poop deck of the boats, on the afternoon of the first massing of troops along the Pasig River; and finally, the flag erect and splendid on the night of that day which was filled for us with anxiety and astonishment.

Spain! Spain! Only the egoistical imbecility that does not understand sacrifice can be ignorant of the enthusiasm and melancholy which that stifled shout coming from far away brought to my mind.

I recalled the list of men who had been sacrificed and my imagination took me back to the piles of dead men who on that night would sleep the eternal sleep under the shining of those same stars that I saw shining through the blinds of my room. Spain! Spain! I recalled the alert sounded by the cordon of sentinels to the right of the river, which guarded the passage of the launches full of wounded men. My imagination conjured up the misfortune visible in the halls of the hospital. I thought I heard the death rattles of dying men during so many nights; the dragging sound of the cart transporting the dead; the slow passage of the Viaticum; the dolorous moans of the men who had suffered amputations, and the quartering of their members that were taken, still palpitating, to be buried on the shores of the river.

Farther off and then closer, the music and cries of enthusiasm came to me; Spain! Spain! The crowds were shouting next to the palace of the Governor General. Ah! Blessed a thousand times are the painful sacrifices made for the fatherland. A righteous mother would kiss and allay with gratitude the tortures inflicted on her sons. The effort was made for something. And the effort had succeeded in having the noble flag, valued by everyone, tremble on the church tower of Imus. In the afternoon, I saw it again, waving in the breeze, pointing to the West, toward the road to the blessed land. And I thought that in that piece of cloth the sons sent the mothers a kiss drenched in the holy blood of sacrifice.

NOTES

1. *Enciclopedia Universal Illustrada* (Barcelona [u.a.]: Hijos de J. Espasa, 1920), vol. 39, 1439, s.v. "Opoponax," refers the reader to the entry "opopónaco de umbelificas." Believed to have medicinal properties since antiquity, a resin-like substance derived from a shrub found mainly in the Middle East and Africa. Used as an antiseptic, an antispasmodic, and an expectorant, it had a bitter flavor and a very strong, aromatic odor.

2. The first battle of Imus, located in Cavite province, took place between August 31–September 3, 1896, shortly after the Katipunan conspiracy was discovered. It marked the first serious defeat of the Spanish Army by rebel troops in the field. In February 1897, General José Lachambre led 9,277 troops to capture Silang, Dasmariñas, Imus, and Bacoor in Cavite. As Ricardo Burguete notes, it was widely believed that a rebel defeat in Imus would be a significant victory for Spanish forces. John Foreman, who was in the Philippines at the time, wrote that the rebels in Imus set fire to the village as the Spaniards approached. Few remained to fight and Imus fell to the Spaniards (Foreman, *The Philippine Islands* (1905), 3rd ed. [London: T. Fisher Unwin, 1906; Project Gutenberg 2007], section 379, http://www.gutenberg.org/ebooks/22815). See Federico Monteverde y Sedano, *Campaña de Filipinas; la división Lachambre 1897* (Madrid: Librería de Hernando y Compañía, 1898), 457–94, for General Lachambre's account of the operation in Imus. He attributed the rebels' retreat to their recognition of superior Spanish forces and firepower. *El Imparcial*, one of the leading newspapers in Spain, proclaimed the "Victoria Decisiva" in Imus on March 28, 1897. Two Spanish reporters were authorized to join the General Staff of the Lachambre Division: Manuel Alhama Montes of *El Imparcial*; Casimiro Franquelo of *El Heraldo* (Monteverde y Sedano, *Campaña*, 150).

Chapter Twenty-Seven

Once the resistance in Imus was defeated, it was necessary to cross the Zapote River, and the forces on each bank began taking Bacoor, Noveleta, Cavite, while the advance troops were pushing back the defeated enemy on the coast and in the cordillera of the Sungay.

During the days it took for the forces to develop their plan, the improvised observatory in the visitors room of the convent served us marvelously well. Day by day we observed the advance of the column, the marches and progress of our offensive actions.

At the end of each day, the Spanish flag waved gloriously on the tower of the conquered town.

At each conquest the townspeople decked themselves out to celebrate the event with music and rockets. The rejoicing seemed to affect the austerity of the convent. In the smiling faces of the Fathers and in the frequent trips to the room that served as an observatory, I thought I saw the severe solemnity that characterized the halls of the convent break down. A discreet and mundane happiness arose from the street and the frequent visits of the daily messengers of news filled everyone with joy.

The dining room abounded in flowers and from that day forward on our initiative there was never lacking a bouquet to hang at the bottom of the pictures that represented the most sublime heroism: heroism that shuns fame gained through sacrifice and the willing surrender of life.

The scent of the flowers in the pleasant dining room perfumed the posthumous lives of those saints, born to end in martyrdom, done with harvesting thorns. The shipwrecked Father; the missionary dressed like a fakir; the venerable old man tormented by fire; all of them lived on in those pictures and all of them received the perfumed gift, a tribute of our admiration awakened by another analogous heroism, by that heroism that every day succumbed there below amidst streams of blood in order to raise a symbol, a flag: the greatest symbol there is after the sacrosanct symbol of the cross.

One day, news arrived at the convent that the General in Chief[1] was going to return to the Peninsula in the first mail ship.

The news was accurate. From then on the advance was paralyzed and it was confirmed that the General's return to the Peninsula was a fact.

On the doctor's advice I was to return on the same mail ship because the complete recovery from my wound would be long and required the therapeutic use of thermal waters. The doctor gave permission for me to go out onto the street. And from the afternoon in which permission was granted I proceeded to prepare for the voyage.

I wanted to bid farewell to the outskirts of Manila in the afternoons I had free from preparations for the trip. I rode alone again in a coach through the sweet-smelling roads lined with chalets and enchanting gardens. One afternoon I returned in an emotional state to the hospital where I passed through all the halls where pain and the interminable vigils of days and nights made the agitated men toss about in their beds. I returned to my old room, a place of refuge for new afflictions. I observed that the new man was sleeping, though he was sweaty and panting, and I left without making a sound, observing the reddish knots on the wood of the windows that, like me, were looking at the wounded sleeper. The knots were like implacable, bloody pupils, which, unblinking, were weeping big tears of resin.

At nightfall I invariably returned to the Malecón. Following in turn the line of coaches, I entered the promenade and saw in passing the animated faces of the excessive gathering of people from one and the other extreme of the central massif, while in the kiosk the musicians played lively songs. The lanterns on the boats in the port stood out like stars of a colossal magnitude. The "Leon XII," which was to take us home, was anchored there. Among the dense shadows one could barely make out as an enormous and blurred mass a foreshortened view of the transatlantic steamer.

Not even one bonfire lit up the coasts of Cavite. Turning back, on the small square where the executions had taken place, a silence of unfathomable and mysterious contrition weighed heavily on the atmosphere.

Back in the convent, we men gathered around the table in the evening. The Brothers, pleased by our appetite and good humor, tried hard, despite their smiling eyes, to look severe when our conversation abused references to *opopanax* and the warm, rosy flesh of Eve.

Chapter Twenty-Seven

NOTE

1. Ricardo Burguete's apparent circumspection regarding the General in Chief was so great that he omitted his name—Camilo García de Polavieja. Polavieja (1838–1914) arrived in the Philippines on December 3, 1896. On December 8 he was named Governor General, Captain General and General in Chief of the Spanish Army, replacing General Ramón Blanco y Erenes. Three months later he resigned, citing ill health as the reason for his departure. His request for more troops and materiel had been denied by the government—a possible factor in his decision. Some contemporaries criticized him for his refusal to grant a pardon to José Rizal, the Chinese mestizo physician and writer, who was on trial for treason when Polavieja arrived. There was speculation that Rizal's connection to Freemasonry provoked the "Christian general's" animus toward the man who became the National Hero. As Burguete notes below, he left for Spain on the same ship as Polavieja on April 15, 1897. For details on Polavieja's role in Rizal's execution, see *The Trial of Rizal* (W. E. Retana's Transcription of the Official Spanish Documents), ed., trans., and anno. Horacio de la Costa, S.J. (Manila: Ateneo de Manila University Press, 1996).

Figure 1. "Lantana," is a small cannon used by Filipino forces against the Spaniards. *Source*: Federico Monteverde y Sedano, *Campaña de Filipinas; la división Lachambre 1897* (Madrid: Librería de Hernando y Compañía, 1898), 77.

Figure 2. Chinese transport worker. Chinese workers were hired or at times conscripted by the Spanish forces. *Source*: Federico Monteverde y Sedano, *Campaña de Filipinas; la división Lachambre 1897* (Madrid: Librería de Hernando y Compañía, 1898), 301.

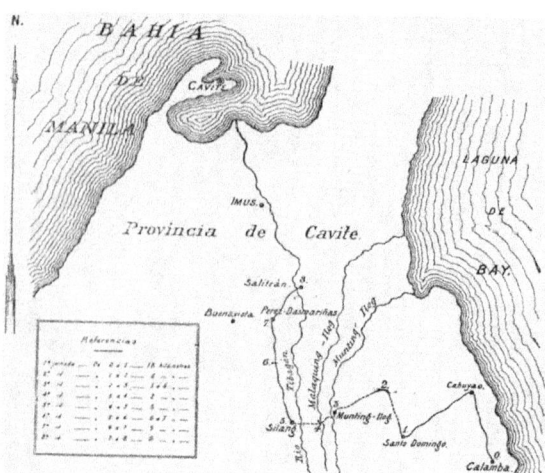

Figure 3. Map of Cavite Province. *Source*: Federico Monteverde y Sedano, *Campaña de Filipinas; la división Lachambre 1897* (Madrid: Librería de Hernando y Compañía, 1898), 423.

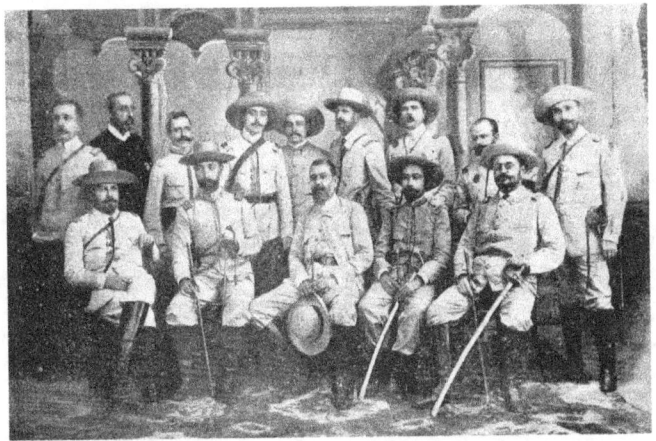

Figure 4. General Lachambre and his General Staff. ***Source*****: Federico Monteverde y Sedano,** ***Campaña de Filipinas; la división Lachambre 1897*** **(Madrid: Librería de Hernando y Compañía, 1898), 431.**

DESDE MANILA

28 marzo 1897

LA VICTORIA DECISIVA

Relato completo del triunfo de Imus

De acuerdo con las instrucciones que habíamos trasmitido á nuestro querido compañero el Sr. Alhama Montes, nos envía por el cable minuciosa y fidelísima relación de las gloriosas jornadas que han destruido el núcleo más importante de los insurrectos, enarbolando la bandera española en la iglesia de Imus.

Lejos de escatimar el peligro, nuestros oficiales se han puesto siempre á la cabeza de las tropas, alcanzando un triunfo tan señalado que puede reputarse como definitivo.

Los telegramas del Sr. Alhama Montes que insertamos á continuación, nos enorgullecen como españoles por las acciones hermosísimas que narran, y como periodistas, por haber logrado, sean los que fueren los sacrificios, honrar estas columnas con el relato de hazañas y proezas que renuevan los más señalados laureles militares de España.

(Por el cable)

De nuestro redactor-corresponsal

(VIA TEHERAN)

MANILA 28 (5,20 tarde)
» » (5,45 »)
» » (11,55 noche)
» 27 (3,50 »)

Camino de Imus

Acaban de llegar los corresponsales señores Conde y Barroso, á quienes tenía encargado que acompañasen á la columna Lachambre.

Estos señores me facilitan los siguientes datos, con los cuales logro hacer un relato completo de las operaciones realizadas.

El miércoles—dice el Sr. Barroso—salimos de la casa-hacienda de Salitrán. Avanzamos yendo tres brigadas por tres caminos distintos.

Llegamos á la trinchera de Anabo, la misma donde murió gloriosamente el general Zabala.

Los rebeldes habían vuelto á ocuparla y habíanla fortalecido con nuevas obras de defensa.

Hallamos en esta trinchera, que los insurrectos conocen ya por la trinchera del general Zabala, tenaz resistencia.

Con las fortificaciones complementarias que han hecho los tagalos, resultaba muy difícil de tomar esta posición.

Tiene á un lado un camino, y al otro barrancos de gran profundidad.

Como no podía pasarse por otro lado, dióse orden de ataque, y las tropas, con gran heroísmo, lanzáronse al asalto por tres distintos puntos á la vez.

Mantúvose el fuego por algún rato.

Cayeron de nuestro lado algunos muertos y bastantes heridos, pero no fué esto obstáculo para que los soldados, al grito de ¡viva España! asaltaran la trinchera.

Una vez en ella, prosiguióse el combate, pues los rebeldes seguían defendiéndose.

A poco de entrar en la posición vióse á un rebelde herido, que tenía insignias de coloríneo en la bocamanga de una chaqueta blanca.

Ahuyentados, por fin, los insurrectos de la trinchera, ordenóse que aquel rebelde herido fuera curado.

Interrogáronle varios oficiales, y dijo llamarse Crispulo Aguinaldo y ser teniente general.

Tenía la herida en el pecho, y cuando el médico estaba sondeándola, dijo el herido:

—Es inútil. Yo muero.

Con efecto; momentos después, el titulado teniente general dejó de existir.

En el asalto de esta trinchera quedaron gravemente heridos los tenientes de caballería D. Constantino Grund, ayudante del general Marina, D. Juan Pérez Igual y don Miguel García Pascual.

Fueron trasportados en camillas al hospital de sangre, donde fallecieron á los pocos minutos de llegar.

Los tres bravos é infortunados oficiales murieron sin recobrar el conocimiento.

Fueron heridos los capitanes de infantería Sres. Ruiz, Gonzalez, el médico D. Aureliano Rodriguez y 101 soldados.

Otra trinchera

El jueves avanzamos en el mismo orden ya dicho, y á los dos kilómetros de marcha hallamos una nueva trinchera como la de Anabo, protegida por los barrios de Imus Lumambayan y Tansanluma.

Esta trinchera estaba oculta por los vallados de las casas. Así fué que nuestras tropas llegaron hasta muy corta distancia sin advertir la defensa de los tagalos.

En una descarga cerrada que éstos hicieron murieron los capitanes Sres. Salgado y Sánchez Minguez, el teniente D. Francisco Ortiz y 22 individuos de tropa.

Causaron esta descarga y sus terribles resultados el natural desconcierto en nuestras tropas.

El teniente de la compañía Sr. Monasterio, á quien correspondía el mando muertos los dos capitanes citados, arengó á las tropas con gran energía, poniéndose á la cabeza de ellas, y gritando ¡Viva España! lanzóse al reducto seguido de todos los nuestros.

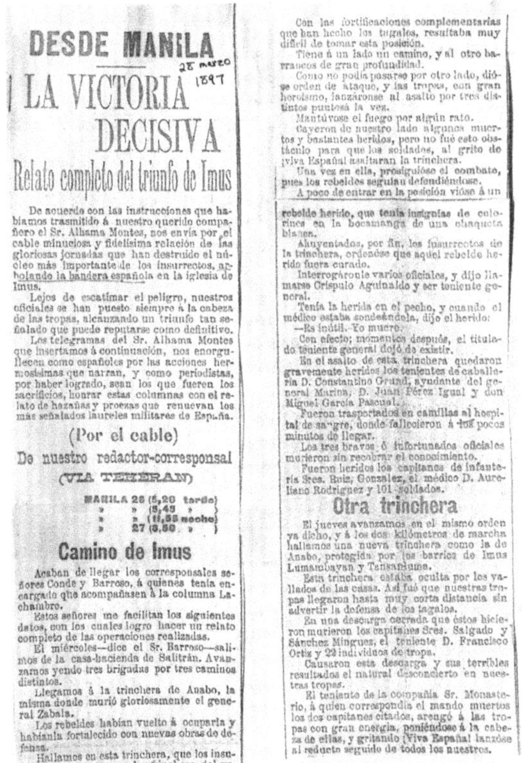

Figure 5. "Victory at Imus." ***Source*****:** ***El Imparcial*** **(Madrid), March 28, 1897.**

Chapter Twenty-Eight

Very early in the morning I heard Mass in the church and took leave of the good Fathers, the indefatigable doctor, and my companions in the convent.

The sun was smiling on the façade of the convent palace and the windows of my room when I turned around from the street to look and say goodbye to those ancient walls that bade me farewell, vibrating now with the high-pitched, melodious psalmody intoned by the voices of the organ inside the church. I felt tender gratitude at the memory of that familiar, well-known voice that wafted into my hearing ineffable caresses that awakened me during the mornings of my convalescence.

On the deck of the "León XIII" that was aiming its prow in the direction of our exit route, I stretched out on a wicker chair and from one side of the ship I watched the arrival of generals, the staff officers, sick and wounded soldiers who constituted the passengers on board.

I recalled my return from Cuba. On that voyage also we carried a rosary of unfortunate dying men. God knows how many beads and strings we must have left en route.

The ship left in mid afternoon. I took one last look at Manila. How many things had happened in little more than half a year!

The walled city lifted its towers and cupolas into space. More to the left, the brightness of the shining zinc roof of the hospital hurt my eyes and the fiery glare off its roof seemed to me to be the reflection of the misfortune that in those hours would sear the bloody bodies of the wounded men. Farther along toward the right, the white walls of the Paco cemetery brought to mind the memory of my good friend Argüelles, asleep in a niche facing the mail route of the fatherland that he had no hope of ever seeing again.

The ship was traversing the bay and the sight of places I knew evoked events that transpired there. Manila was no longer visible. Now we were leaving behind the Ensenada of Pampanga. I remembered the little house of Sr. N. . . . his illness, his bad omens, and I saw in my mind's eye the weeping figures of the orphans in mourning. What must have become of them?

The mountain range of Bataan surged into view. I recalled my first days along and across that steep mountain range.

When night fell we sailed around the point of Marivales leaving the island of Corregidor on the left. I stood up to take leave of the western beach that extended until it was lost to sight. Bagac, Morón were points scarcely perceptible to the senses but my memory saw them clearly as I called them to mind. My thought quickly focused on the sight of the piece of wood, fixed in the sand and kissed by the waves that guarded the bodies of the dead soldiers from my company. Life's shipwrecked men, all of them, protector and protected, slept the eternal sleep in a tight bundle and received with the tides the ensuing, unforgettable kiss of the pious waters.

As in Cuba, the entire Archipelago was covered with graves that—as in the Fatherland—did not have commemorative monuments. Forgetfulness of the glorious victims left behind in Jolo, Mindanao and in all of the Archipelago since the conquest would weigh equally on the men sacrificed in the current campaign.

In the future the wind and water would kiss the graves dug out in the forest lands and in the sands of the beaches.

The coast faded from sight. We were entering the China Sea and the León "XIII" moved proudly over the slightly ruffled sea, cutting through the foam of the indolent, idle waves.

Chapter Twenty-Nine

The journey was sad and painful for me. It was impossible to leave the ship at the various ports of call without risk to my recovery. I distracted myself with memories during the long stops the ship made in ports where it took on coal.

During the last three weeks of the voyage I immersed my sad glances alternately in the sea and in space. For three nights the same dream troubled me and ended by tormenting my imagination during the day.

I dreamed the first time one night after attending the sad ceremony of casting overboard a poor employee who died devoured by fever and anemia contracted in the Philippines after three long years of labor.

In between dreams I saw my friend Argüelles and Sr. N . . ., each of whom showed me the reality of their prophecies which I had interpreted as pessimism.

All our efforts had been useless and all the blood shed was sterile. The Spanish state deceived itself; it seemingly extinguished the fires of the war, but out of neglect left an ember that was ignited by winds blowing in from unknown directions, thereby propagating the fire throughout all the islands. The Archipelago was no longer ours. The nation, seeing the approaching catastrophe draw near, relinquished its sovereignty and, with a *"sauve qui peut,"* abandoned its children.

Few had managed to escape and the majority, forgotten by the nation, dragged on a miserable life of slavery under the dominion of the *indios*, exchanged on a daily basis for death. I saw in my dreams the little house of Sr. N . . . reduced to ashes. The poor old man half dead, sitting in the midst of the burned wood of his dwelling . . . His daughters . . . Oh! His daughters were carried off by insurgent bands and were never heard of again. On the wings of my dreams I returned to all the places I had frequented . . . It was another country for me, another land on which the remains of a ragged army, abandoned and conquered, worked without respite, submitted to the beatings of the conqueror, who demanded that they rebuild the ruins. On the towers where once the flag of the fatherland was raised with pride and glory I now saw the Katipunan flag floating in the air, raised amid tears and blows by those same trembling skeletons that one day, in order to raise the ensign of Spain gladly gave the blood from their veins at the foot of those towers. Over open scars the bruises appeared from the blows with which the hangmen punished the exhaustion or resistance of those ragged platoons in which chiefs, officers and soldiers were mixed up together . . . No redemption or hope was possible. The cruelty of the hangmen increased when they learned about the abandonment in which the nation was leaving those poor wretches. Seeing how their country abandoned them, God knows how they had been recruited! Down with that horde! Get rid of those mountains of flesh abandoned by their own . . .

Invariably, keen indignation awakened me from my dream. Spain! Spain! I recalled the enthusiastic cry of the troops returning from combat to aerate the piles of the dead and cool the burning foreheads of the wounded men. It was not possible. But after dreaming for three consecutive nights, once I awakened, the horrible history had the force and the fixity of an omen. No, no it wasn't possible. The efforts made by Spain for four centuries to conquer the Archipelago passed before my imagination. I recalled all the expeditions[1]: the first led by Magellan; the second by Loaisa; the expedition of Saavedra sent to save the handful of Spaniards who had survived the previous expedition, defending themselves heroically in a fort on the coast. The expedition of Villalobos followed, then that of Legazpi up to the successful domination of the country. Such was the effort Spain put into the conquest and such was the manner in which it recruited men and money to save men lost in voyages that these expeditions began to take on the character of a crusade. Neither greed, prosperity or commerce were behind these efforts; the noble idea of rescuing captive brothers motivated those troops of soldiers who, if they could have joined the means at their disposal with their desires, would have recruited soldiers from the smallest villages and poorest hamlets in the Peninsula.

No, it was not possible. And in my moments of sadness, struggling against the anxiety produced by my dream, I submerged my anguished gaze into the unsounded depth of the ocean or into the diaphanous blue of the cloudless, merciful sky.

No, it was not possible. It was enough to abandon the dead in Cuba, asleep in the bottom of swamps, by the side of roads on the edges of forests, alongside those of men recently abandoned on the coasts of the Archipelago and with those who at the end of the campaign we sowed in the sea like a string of beads in a rosary that would unite the metropolis with the colony in the East.

But abandon the living? Never, never. The legendary land of the Crusades, the land that century after century gave blood to rescue captives. What colossal effort would it not undertake to rescue our brothers?

Logic and reason erased the distress caused by the dream and in the last days of the voyage, close to the coast of Spain, as I breathed in breezes saturated in the aromatic bosom of the land, I thought about the felicitous results of the campaign. I was hopeful about the coming triumph and, determined to shake off the dreams and deliriums of a sick man, I picked up my crutches one afternoon, within sight of Cerdeña, and strove to maintain my balance, and taking baby steps . . . for the first time, I walked about the deck.

NOTE

1. Burguete recalls notable expeditions by the men named here. Ferdinand Magellan (1489–1521) was a Portuguese explorer who was killed before the completion of the circumnavigation of the earth by the Spanish expedition he headed to the East Indies (1519–1522). García Jofre de Loaísa (1490–1526) was ordered by Charles I of Spain to colonize the Spice Islands. Alvaro de Saavedra Cerón's (?–1529) expedition (1527–1529) was to find out what had happened to the survivors of the Magellan, Cabot, and Loaísa expeditions. He reached Mindanao where he rescued two survivors of the Magellan expedition. Ruy López de Villalobos (c1500–1544) was sent in 1543 to reach the Philippines. When he reached Mindanao in that year he conferred the name "Filipinas" (in honor of Crown Prince Philip) on the archipelago. Miguel López de Legazpi (1565–1572) established a settlement in what was to become Manila in 1571. He ordered the construction of the walled city of Intramuros. The settlement was proclaimed the island's capital and the seat of the government in the East Indies. Legazpi became the first Spanish governor of the Philippines.

Chapter Thirty

Consummatum est

Since the period when certain events transpired and the present as I transcribe them, time has passed sometimes quickly, at times slowly.[1]

The catastrophe foreseen in my confused dreams came about in the end. From the little country house perched on the slopes of the mountains on the outskirts of Barcelona, I try to sort out my memories. They pass onto these pages burned perhaps by the incandescent fire of indignation and enthusiasm.

Standing on the white terrace of my house, completely cured and restored from my wounds, there is not a single afternoon when—as I contemplate the vast extension of Barcelona stretched out at my feet and lift my sight to the port with its masts and the broad extension of the sea that the horizon encloses,—I do not think about the happy afternoon of my departure for the Archipelago and that other fortunate afternoon when I returned to Spain.

Time has transpired for me either quickly or slowly, but in the long succession of days not one day has passed when I have failed to dedicate a memory to the companions who left in the afternoon from the same port I'm looking at now filled with pride and joy to defend the rights of a mother who turned out to be sufficiently vile to keep on living after abandoning them.

There down below some remained; over there, still others; in the Indies of the East and the Indies of the West. It was no longer one sea: it was two seas, the Eastern and the Western sea that were keeping count of the dead like the beads of a rosary in the depths of their merciful refuge.

Spain! Spain!

The stimulating cry that revived the dying men returning from Cuba, the cry that in the Indian Ocean made our veins swell with enthusiasm, the cry on the return from battle in the mouths of the ardent soldiers who kissed the bloody pile of the dead and the burning foreheads of the wounded men:

Spain! Spain!

The silent cry of dying men; at the foot of the parapets; along the swamps; in the depths of the forest; in the hold of ships:

Spain! Spain!

The cry that made it possible to withstand causes of distress in the hospital; thirst, hunger, questions of *justice*. That cry which was once transporting for me, now reaches my ears with an infinite melancholy, with an aftertaste of bitterness and sadness . . . Spain! Spain!

There is still time. There is something left to do for the country. I am setting it out here in a work that I am copying and which I summarize in this sentence:

GLORY TO THE DEAD!

"All of the foreign press echoed the beautiful ceremony presided over by Emperor William, on the inauguration of the glorious, commemorative statue of the first regiment of the Guard.[2]

The celebration was moving and eloquent, and the discourse of William II was no less so.

On the same soil that drank the blood of the former comrades of the regiment, the first regiment of the Guard won the honor of parading at the head, and amid the troops' *hurra*s! and the blast of the batteries' one hundred eleven discharges, the regiment flew the glorious flags of the 70th and 71st. When they marched before the statue that represents the Archangel St. Michael, they lowered their lances until they kissed the ground. The ground was made sacrosanct by the blessed blood of heroism!

A worthy tribute and a glorious homage rendered to the dead, with no distinction between friends and enemies. The Emperor said as much at the end of his superb discourse . . . `I want this statue, dedicated to the regiment-school of the Hohenzollern to convey universal significance. Upon this soil drenched in blood this bronze statue is raised to commemorate the death of all the brave men who succumbed in combat, French soldiers as well as our own. Death covers with glory the conqueror and the conquered alike. And when our flags bend down and, unfurled, salute the commemorative statue, they float in melancholy fashion over the graves of glorious ancestors, but they will also salute and bend down before those of our adversaries because this homage is equally due to all who succumbed in the fight."

"A beautiful speech! A moving ceremony that caused an emotional reaction visible in the men's faces and, following a sudden deafening burst of cannon, momentarily drowned out the virile and potent *hurras!* of the soldiers.

As I read this account, the memory of our recent misfortunes came forcefully to my imagination and, as is logical, there came to mind the long string of such events over the entire century.

Chapter Thirty

Our disasters are passing into History; the dead into oblivion. And as if death did not encircle with laurel the temples of the dead in the field of battle, conquerors and conquered, our egoism leads us to throw a thick veil over the disasters so that we obscure the memory of those brothers who, on the altar of duty or enthusiasm, and free of responsibility for the poor direction or wretched conditions of combat, paid on the field of battle the most sublime tribute that men can pay.

There is no monument in Spain from the campaign in Santo Domingo up to the present that commemorates the sacrifice of those who succumbed in our civil or colonial wars.

The same thing will happen in the present.

Governments that boast of programs of regeneration do not include the work of glorifying the memory of dead soldiers in their own programs. Among us, this work—undertaken with great effort by the heads of other states—does not merit even a moment of attention.

France commemorates a monument to each one of its defeats; and there where it does not win the laurel of victory, mourning crepe serves as a tribute and remembrance.

We shall forget again in Spain. Along swamps, in the depths of forests, along the sides of roads, the remains of those who fell in combat will sleep eternally, and in this nation there will be not be any remembrance nor will they be rendered any tribute other than that offered by isolated family piety, a tribute dedicated not to the soldier but to the loved one.

If we are to begin the task of regeneration, let us start by glorifying the dead and erecting a simple tomb of perpetual memory.

Piety should hasten to emend the forgetfulness of a government; let someone initiate this pious work by organizing a subscription. And if the harshness of recent blows has numbed the nation's sensibility, let the army itself undertake the task for it has more than enough resources. It can head this subscription by using one day's payment given to all army pensioners to glorify the memory of those who, losing along with their lives all rights to recompense, may, as is exceptional and just, live perpetually in the memory of the living."

Let each one comply with his duty in this task of repentance and reform . . .

I have complied with mine and I make my sons comply with it as well. Without a monument where we can pray and render tribute, today, tomorrow and always for the sake of tradition—if I succeed in transmitting the tradition to my grandchildren—my offspring will pray as they do now at the feet of a crucifix of redemption, decorated with a bit of the country's flag . . . They pray for the *"manes"* [spirits] of the glorious dead: for my brother, for my companions, for my soldiers . . . for Spain, in short . . . And the cry that one afternoon enflamed my soldiers and caused the hair of my head to stand up on my head as we buried our first dead under a path on that distant and sacrosanct beach—that cry electrifies my little ones and leads them in turn to cry out at the foot of their Christ, of their King, and their flag the first name they learned to babble:

—Spain! Spain!

Barcelona, September 1900

NOTES

1. On *Consummatum est.*, see n14 of the Introduction.
2. Wilhelm II, Emperor of Germany (1859–1941).

Bibliography

Agoncillo, Teodoro A. *Revolt of the Masses: The Story of Bonifacio and the Katipunan*. Quezon City: University of the Philippines, 1956.

Balfour, Sebastian. *The End of the Spanish Empire, 1898–1923*. Oxford: Clarendon Press, 1997.

Blanco, Manuel, with Pedro G. Galende. *Flora de Filipinas*. Reissue of the grand edition of 1877–1883. 3 vols. Manila: San Augustín Convent, 1993.

Blasco Ibáñez, Vicente. *Artículos contra la Guerra en Cuba*. Edited by J. L. León Roca. Valencia: León Roca, 1978.

Bonoan, Raul J., S.J. *The Rizal-Pastells Correspondence: The Hitherto Unpublished Letters of José Rizal and Portions of Fr. Pablo Pastell's Fourth Letter and Translation of the Correspondence, Together with a Historical Background and Theological Critique*. Manila: Ateneo de Manila University Press, 1994.

Cabana, Francesc. *La burguesía catalana: Una aproximación histórica*. Barcelona: Proa, 1996.

Carlyle, Thomas. *On Heroes, Hero-Worship, and the Heroic in History: Six Lectures*. London: James Fraser, 1841.

Costa, Horacio de la, S.J., ed. and trans. *The Trial of Rizal* (W. E. Retana's Transcription of the Official Spanish Documents). Manila: Ateneo de Manila University Press, 1996.

Del Pilar, Marcelo H. *Monastic Supremacy in the Philippines*. Translated by Encarnación Alzona. Quezon City: Philippine Historical Association, 1958.

Enciclopedia Universal Illustrada. Barcelona [u.a.]: Hijos de J. Espasa, 1920.

Filipinas: Problema fundamental por un español de larga residencia en aquellas islas. Madrid: Aguado, 1891.

Foradada, Francisco, S.J. *La Soberanía de España en Filipinas, Opúsculo de Actualidad*. Barcelona: Henrich y Compañía, 1897.

Foreman, John, F.R.G.S. *The Philippine Islands* (1905). 3rd ed. London: T. Fisher Unwin, 1906; Project Gutenberg 2007. Available online at http://www.gutenberg.org/ebooks/22815.

Hernández Sandoica, Elena, and María Fernanda Mancebo. "Higiene y sociedad en la guerra de Cuba (1895-1898): Notas sobre soldados y proletarios." *Estudios de Historia Social* 5-6 (1978): 361-84.

Jensen, R. Geoffrey. *Cultura militar española: Modernistas, tradicionalistas y liberales*. Madrid: Biblioteca Nueva, 2014.

———. *Irrational Triumph: Cultural Despair, Military Nationalism, and the Ideological Origins of Franco's Spain*. Reno: University of Nevada Press, 2002.

———. "Recepción literaria y cultura bélica: la generación del 98, Ricardo Burguete y el nacionalismo militar en España." *Bulletin of Spanish Studies* 84, no. 7 (2007): 871–88.

Kalaw, Teodoro M. *La masonería filipina: Su origen, desarrollo y vicisitudes hasta la época presente*. Manila: Bureau of Printing, 1920.

———. *La Revolución Filipina/The Philippine Revolution*. Manila: Manila Book Co., [1925].

Macaulay, Thomas Babington. "Lord Clive." In *Critical and Historical Essays*. Volume 1. First published 1843; Project Gutenberg 2016. Available online at http://www.gutenberg.org/ebooks/2332.

Monteverde y Sedano, Federico. *Campaña de Filipinas; la división Lachambre 1897*. Madrid: Librería de Hernando y Compañía, 1898.

Mount, Ferdinand. Review "Umbrageousness." *London Review of Books* 39, no. 17 (September 7, 2017): 3–8.

Pellico, Silvio. *My Ten Years' Imprisonment*. Edited by Henry Morley. Translated by Thomas Roscoe. London: Cassell, 1886; Project Gutenberg 2000. Available online at http://www.gutenberg.org/ebooks/2792.

Puell de la Villa, Fernando. *El Soldado desconocido; De la leva a la "mili" (1700–1912)*. Madrid: Editorial Biblioteca Nueva, 1996.

Republic of the Philippines. "PNR in Philippine History." n.d. Available online at http://www.pnr.gov.ph/about-contact-us/who-we-are/pnr-in-philippine-history/pnr-in-philippine-history.

Ría-Baja, Carlos. *El Desastre Filipino: Memorias de un prisionero*. Barcelona: Tipografía La Académica, de Serra Hermanos y Russell, 1899.

Schumacher, John N., S.J. *Revolutionary Clergy: The Filipino Clergy and the Nationalist Movement, 1850–1903*. Quezon City: Ateneo de Manila University Press, 1981.

Sheehan, James. "Echoes from the Far Side." Review of *The Pursuit of Power: Europe 1815–1914*, by Richard J. Evans. *London Review of Books* 39, no. 20 (October 19, 2017): 21–22.

La Solidaridad. "History of Philippine Masonry." *Philippine Center for Masonic Studies*. n.p. Online at http://www.philippinemasonry.org/philippine-masonry-from-barcelona-to-manila-1889-1896.html.

St. Clair, Francis. *The Katipunan: Or The Rise and Fall of the Filipino Commune*. Manila: Tip. "Amigos del País," Palacio 258, 1902.

Walker, D. J. *Representations of the Cuban and Philippine Insurrections on the Spanish Stage, 1887–1898*. Tempe, AZ: Bilingual Press, 2001.

Zaide, Gregorio F. *Documentary History of the Katipunan Discovery: A crítico-historical study of the Betrayal of the KKK. New Revelations*. 2nd ed. Manila, 1931.

Index

Aden, 28, 29n3, 31, 34; Gulf of, 27; cisterns, 27
Aguinaldo, Emilio, 77
Albuquerque, Afonso de, 19, 23n2
Anda Salazar, Simón de, 53, 55n1
anilloso canuto (boregheh mask), 22, 23n6

black *aetas*, 61; negritos, 63n1, 65, 79n1
Blanco y Erenes, Ramón, 135n1
Blasco Ibáñez, Vicente, 17n1
boregheh mask, 22, 23n6

Cape Guardafui, 28, 29n4
Carlyle, Thomas, xiii, 4, 84, 85n2; *norsos*, 7, 83, 84; Valkyries, 7, 8, 84, 85n2, 91
Chinese brigades, 7, 8, 83, 85n1, 91, 99
cisterns, 27
Clive, Lord Robert, 4, 34, 36n11
coal, 3, 20–21, 37
Colombo, 4, 31; Buddha statue, 32, 33; European quarter, 21, 32; "Mahawanso," 33, 36n6; pagoda, 32; variety of races, 33
conscription, 114n2; recruitment policy, 112, 114n2
Cortés, Hernán, 34, 36n12

De Lesseps, Ferdinand, 19, 23n2

ethnic and racial groups: Abyssinians, 27; Arabs, 21–22; Berbers, 3, 20, 21; Chinese, 5–6, 37, 42, 48n4, 79n1; diversity in Colombo, 4; Egyptians, 3, 20; Ethiopians, 3, 20, 21; Europeans, 4; Hindu (as a race), 33; *indios*, 33, 41–42, 45, 50, 53–54, 79n1; Jews, 21–22; Spanish, 79n1
expeditions to the Philippines, 142; de Legazpi, Miguel López, 142, 143n1; de Loaisa, García Jofre, 142; de Saavedra Cerón, Alvaro, 142, 143n1; de Villlalobos, Ruy López, 142, 143n1; Magellan, Ferdinand, 142, 143n1

flags, 2, 38, 39, 43, 53, 69, 127, 131; British, 27; noble flag, 132; in Singapore, 3; Spanish, xii, 2, 12, 82, 98, 113, 133
friars, 2, 10–11, 11–12, 43, 47, 48n6, 49, 52n1, 113n1

Galván [Galvao], Duarte, 19, 23n2

Imus victory, 129, 132n2

Jesuits, 10–11, 13n12, 124

Katipunan, 8, 10, 12, 12n1, 49–50
khamsin (winds), 25–26

Legazpi, Miguel López de, 5, 43, 48, 142, 143n1

Macaulay, Thomas Babington, 4, 34, 36n11; on Lord Clive, 4, 34, 36n11
Maldives. *See* Socotora [Socotra]
Masonic power, 111, 113–14
mestizos, 42, 48n4, 79n1
Mount Ophir, 37, 40n1

negritos, 63n1, 65, 79n1
Nicobar Islands, 35, 36n13

Peak of Adán, 34, 36n10
Pellico, Silvio, 116
Peris, [Perim]: island of, 27, 29n2
Pizarro, Francisco, 34, 36n12
Polavieja, Camilo García De, 135n1
Port Said, 3–4, 16, 19, 21, 23n1, 25; diversity of races and ethnic groups, 4; downloading coal, 3; mosque, 22; orchestra, 21; quarters, 21; shops, 21

racial groups. *See* ethnic and racial groups
regeneration, 12, 14n15, 147
religious orders, 111; Jesuits, 10–11, 13n12, 124

Sepoys, 38, 40n3
Singapore, 37, 40n2; Sepoys, 38, 40n3
Socotora [Socotra], 31, 35n1
Spanish expeditions to the Philippines, 142
Suez Canal, 3–5, 15, 19, 23n1

Tondo (early name for Manila), 41, 48n1
Tonkin, 34, 36n9

Volapuk, 21, 23n5

Walker, D. J., xii
William II, Emperor, 12, 146

About the Editor

D. J. Walker is professor emerita at the University of New Orleans, and the author of *Representations of the Cuban and Philippine Insurrections on the Spanish Stage, 1887–1898* (Bilingual Press, 2001); *Spanish Women and the Colonial Wars of the 1890s* (Louisiana State University Press, 2008); and *Crime at El Escorial: The 1892 Child Murder, the Press, and the Jury* (International Scholars, 1994; rev. ed. University Press of America, 2014). She has also published three translations: *On Captivity. A Spanish Soldier's Experience in a Havana Prison, 1896–1898*, by Manuel Ciges Aparicio (University of Alabama Press, 2012); *Nan Dòmi: An Initiate's Journey into Haitian Vodou*, by Mimerose P. Beaubrun (City Lights Books, 2013); and *Memoir of My Youth in Cuba. A Spanish Soldier in the Spanish Army during the Separatist War, 1895–1898*, by Josep Conangla (University of Alabama Press, 2017).

www.ingramcontent.com/pod-product-compliance
Lightning Source LLC
Chambersburg PA
CBHW052049300426
44117CB00012B/2046